SITTING BULL SPOKE

The chiefs sat around the council fire awaiting Sitting Bull's final instructions.

"Swift riders will go at once to every hunting band of Indians yet free upon the prairies. At the same time, riders will go to every agency of the Sioux, Cheyenne and Arapaho to the sunward of the Big Muddy River. The riders will whip their ponies hard. When the ponies stagger at last into the prairie camps and the agency villages, the riders will leap from their backs and will rip open the entry-flaps of each chief's tipi, speaking to him these words of Tatanka Yotanka:

"*'It is war. Come to the camp of Sitting Bull which then will be at the big bend of the Rosebud River. Let us all get together and have one more big fight with the soldiers!'*"

"*Hun-hun-he!*" roared the chiefs, deep voices bounding from the buffalo skins of the council lodge. "Let us die as proud men, as free men, as Indians—!"

D0827650

CUSTER'S LAST STAND

WILL HENRY

BANTAM BOOKS
TORONTO · NEW YORK · LONDON · SYDNEY

For
KIN PLATT
old friend
and true

*This low-priced Bantam Book
has been completely reset in a type face
designed for easy reading, and was printed
from new plates. It contains the
text of the original hard-cover edition.*

CUSTER'S LAST STAND

*A Bantam Book / published by arrangement with
Chilton Book Co.*

PRINTING HISTORY

Chilton edition published September 1966

Bantam edition / September 1982

ISBN 0-553-22684-3

Published simultaneously in the United States and Canada

PRINTED IN THE UNITED STATES OF AMERICA

O   0 9 8 7 6 5 4 3 2 1

FOREWORD

This is the true story of General George Armstrong Custer and the Battle of the Little Big Horn. Known in myth and legend as "Custer's Last Stand," this battle was unquestionably the greatest Cavalry and Indian fight in the history of the American frontier. Yet its story has been told in more wrong ways than any other adventure of the Western past.

The events depicted herein are drawn from the actual documents of the times, and from eye-witness testimonies of the Indians who lived then, both Sioux and Cheyenne.

Certain conversations and descriptions have been supplied by the author where the silent tongues of the dead, red man and white, could not speak for themselves.

The essential facts are faithful, alike, to the heroic memories of the gallant officers and men of the Seventh U.S. Cavalry, and to the valiant red horsemen who rode against them in the name of freedom on that June day in 1876, in far Montana.

W.H.

Custer Battlefield
Little Big Horn
Montana, 1965

CONTENTS

Part Four–THE ROSEBUD

Part Five–THE LITTLE BIG HORN

PART ONE

THE WASHITA

1. THE CAMP OF BLACK KETTLE

The Seventh Cavalry moved toward the sleeping Indian encampment like a hungry wolf, silently in the dead of the winter night. In a snow-filled gully behind low hills, General Custer halted his command. The breaths of men and of horses rose in frosty silver columns in the biting cold. The jingle of harness, the squeaking of saddle leather—these were the only sounds.

Beyond the hills lay the Washita River and the tipis of the unsuspecting Cheyenne, Arapaho and Kiowa tribes gathered together there to spend the Time of the Deep Snows where all would be safe, warm, happy.

True, there had been bad fighting with the white Pony Soldiers that past summer of 1868. Nor did the red men deny their part of the blame. But all of that was behind them now.

Far to the north their Sioux brother, Red Cloud, had just touched the pen—made a new treaty—with the Great Father in Washington. The treaty promised peace. Word of it swept to the south, even to the banks of the Washita. Black Kettle and the other chiefs of the three tribes resting there gave thanks and prayed to their red gods in gratitude. They told their people that now all would be well. They might close their eyes in safety at last. The Pony Soldiers would come no more.

But beyond the low hills that black November night, the Seventh Cavalry lay waiting in the snow with no thought to the new treaty. General Custer had orders other than those of peace. He had been sent on this winter march to find the Indians when their ponies were weak from lack of grass and could not escape the grain-fed strong horses of the cavalry troops. When he found the Indians, his orders were to destroy them, to scatter them, to drive them back upon the reservations —whatever he could do to them. But in no event was he to allow them to escape, to get away and go free.

The Indians were much at fault. They knew this. In August, on the Solomon River, they had killed fifteen white people. They had carried off five innocent white women. They had raided on the Saline River, killing more. They had also killed settlers on the Republican River. In September, they had burned a wagon train and seventeen men at Cimarron Crossing. They had murdered six men near Fort Wallace. At Spanish Fork, they had killed four men, outraged three women, brutally murdered four small children before their parents' eyes. These were terrible things—evil things. But many of the Indians said that they did them only because the whites had done so much evil to the red man. Others among them made no excuses, and were sad in their hearts, and guilty.

Doing evil for evil, they said, made all men bad.

For his part, General George Armstrong Custer was no Indian hater. He admired the red man. He said, always, that he was a brave and noble foe, and driven to many of his crimes by the misdoings of the white men in his lands.

But Custer was first of all things a soldier.

And a soldier obeyed his orders.

Now, to his dimly lighted tent, Custer called all of his officers and his scouts. Lieutenant Tom Custer, the General's younger brother, was there. Captain Benteen was there. And the names of the scouts read like a roll-call of frontier legends: Apache Bill, California Joe, Ben Clark, the Mexican half-breed "Romero," and the Osage Indian "Hard Rope." They were men who, as the saying went, "could track a hive of white bees through a blizzard." Yet, strangely, on this dark and stormy night they were all lost—or so Custer accused them of being when all had gathered and were waiting.

"Gentlemen," said the famous officer, "I want to suggest that not one of you knows where he is! All of your great and fabled reputations mean nothing. You are fortunate that your commander happens to own a compass, and knows how to read its arrow, even in the dark!"

Custer spoke with a nervous, quick grin. His voice was high and excitable. He was a friendly man, but severe on bunglers. Moreover, he was a very proud man and loved to demonstrate to others his own superiority.

"At least we know," he said, holding up the compass for all to see its needle, "that we are still on our due-south course, and cannot be overly far from the Indians."

Here the little withered Osage stepped forward. He held up his dark hand, shaking his head. "Compass no have ears," he said. "Injun do."

Custer knew that the small scout had more to say. The General was a keen student of the red man, and appreciated his ways.

"What do you mean, Hard Rope?" he asked.

"Compass no hear dog bark just now," replied the Osage. "Me do."

"What? In this wind and snow! Are you sure?" Custer was doubtful, but he felt his nerves tighten. The other officers crowded forward.

"Me hear dog bark," insisted the small man. "You come go follow me. Me show you."

"Where?" demanded Custer.

"Past him low hill over there," said Hard Rope. "You go along me, you hear dog, too."

"Gentlemen!" Custer's voice snapped with excitement. "I have a hunch Hard Rope is right. I am going with him. All scouts, forward with us! You—Benteen, Elliott, Gibbs—bring the men forward. Keep in column. No talking, no smoking. Do not get too far behind us, but maintain quiet at all cost!"

He was gone before his officers could discuss or

question the plan. He was Custer. He led. Others merely followed.

"I hope," said one of the staff, "that for a change he knows what he is doing."

"He had better know," said a fellow officer. "Somewhere off there in the night are old Black Kettle and a hundred eighty lodges of southern Cheyenne. That's at least three hundred fifty warriors right there, and the good Lord knows how many more Kiowa and Arapaho braves camped with them. I heard Romero guess at a thousand warriors."

"Well, you know the General," a third officer volunteered, uneasily. "He'll charge them if there's ten thousand."

"Some day," said Captain Benteen, who knew Custer better than any of them, "he's going to *find* his ten thousand Indians. Then we'll all wish we had decided to be something else besides officers and gentlemen in the Seventh Cavalry!"

"Oh, aren't you the cheerful one!" laughed a young lieutenant. "Personally, I think the General could whip those ten thousand redskins, if he ever found them. What do you think of that?"

Captain Benteen paused in the doorwary of the tent. He looked hard at the young lieutenant, then nodded sharply.

"Just what I think of Custer," he said. "You're crazy, too."

2. HARD ROPE HEARS
THE PONY BELLS

Custer held the reins tightly on his horse. Beside him, Hard Rope pointed ahead. The storm was lifting now. The stars glittered. The moonlight, where it shot through the ragged clouds, painted the snows a glaring white. Custer could clearly see the long ridge which lay beyond the low hills. He glanced back, slowing his horse. California Joe and the other scouts also halted. Behind them, two hundred yards away, the cavalry column had also stopped moving forward.

"Is that the elevation you want me to climb with you?" Custer asked Hard Rope.

"Village hide other side ridge," replied the Osage. "Me you climb. You see."

"All right," said Custer. "Come on."

They started ahead. With them went California Joe. The other scouts went back to tell the troops to stay where they were until the General returned.

Hard Rope led the way up the ridge. He went at a snow-crunching trot. Custer and California Joe had difficulty keeping up with him. Atop the ridge, the Osage beckoned for them to lie down beside him. They did so, all three men peering intently into the darkness below.

"I don't see a thing and I don't hear a thing," complained Custer nervously. "You've missed your way, Hard Rope. There's no big Cheyenne village down there."

"Be quiet," said the Indian, showing no fear of the

6

officer's high rank and his fame as a war leader of the white men. "Keep mouth shut, ear open. Aha! There! You hear him dog bark?"

Custer strained his ears. "I hear nothing!" he said. "And I see nothing except that jumble of small hills and river timber there in the big bend of the Washita."

"Listen more hard," commanded the Indian.

Custer started to say something in anger, but California Joe touched his arm. "Begging your pardon, General," the tall white scout said. "But Hard Rope is right. Listen."

This time Custer heard the bark. And then another. And another. Those *were* dogs barking, faint and thin, but very clear now. They could be nothing but Indian dogs in this distant and lonely place. Custer's whisper grew tense.

"But I still don't *see* anything!" he insisted stubbornly.

"You no look right place," muttered Hard Rope. "Me see Cheyenne pony herd right there. Look. Bottom this hill."

"Bah!" said Custer. "Those are buffalo down there!"

"General," said California Joe, "if them are buffalo down there, they're the first buffalo I ever knowed of to wear grazing bells hung on their necks."

"How is that, sir?" demanded Custer sharply. "Are you making fun of me?" His temper was as quick as his famous "peg-toothed grin." But California Joe was not joking.

"No sir, General," he said "Keep listening."

Suddenly, Custer was propping himself up on his elbows, high voice crackling with excitement.

"By heaven, man!" he cried. "I *do* hear pony bells!"

Hard Rope grunted something uncomplimentary in Osage, and came to his feet. California Joe turned to Custer.

"Come on, General," he said. "Bend low and don't talk so loud. We've found your Injuns for you."

The commander of the Seventh Cavalry obeyed the scout's warning. Crouching, he followed California Joe and Hard Rope. But at the last moment he paused atop the snowy crest, peering into the blackness which hid the Indian encampment below. His words were spoken so softly aloud that only the night wind heard them. And only the glitter of the far, high stars lit the moment's triumph in his thin face.

"Sleep well, Black Kettle," he said. "Yellow Hair is coming!"

3. DEATH COMES FOR DOUBLE WOLF

The men prepared for the attack, leaving everything they could behind. Into the snow went their rations of coffee and hardtack, and their saddlebags of oats for the horses. The troopers carried only fighting gear, their readied carbines, a hundred rounds of ammunition. Even their winter overcoats were thrown aside. The man who talked in ranks, now, faced death from the firing squad. The officers and scouts came to Custer's side when all was ready.

"Yellow Hair," as the Indians called him, spoke quickly.

There would be four attack columns. One, under Major Elliott, would swing wide of the Indian camp and attack from the east. One, under Colonel Meyers, would go to the right and attack from the south. Custer and young Captain Thompson would attack from the center, hitting the camp from the west. The river lay to the north and would serve to prevent escape in that direction. Were there any questions?

None of the officers said a word. They only saluted.

"All right," said the General. "Let's be about it, then." He turned to the young officer who would ride with him, his pale blue eyes ablaze with eagerness. "Captain Thompson," he said, "you will hold your command to a walk until we are discovered by the Indians. Good luck."

"Yes sir, General," said the young soldier. "Thank you."

The four hundred horses of the troops of Custer and Thompson started forward. They split in two lines, like the fork of a snake's tongue, to go around the base of the last of the low hills between the advancing cavalry and the Cheyenne village. It was now early in the morning, with the gray light of the new day just staining the hilltops. There was still no sound from the village.

On the far side of the hill a lone tipi stood. From this tipi to the top of the hill ran a narrow path. Up this path, each dawn, went the camp's sentry, leaving his warm guardpost-lodge and his wife for the frost of the daybreak.

All of the Indians knew that Yellow Hair and his Pony Soldiers were somewhere in their country. Black Kettle had said to keep a sharp lookout—had warned the sentry warriors to go very early to their posts. Thus it was that Double Wolf, faithful to his trust, had started up the hill path when behind him he heard a fearful cry. It was his wife.

Turning, he saw the woman come out of the tipi. She was dragging their two small children, still half asleep. She pointed frantically, first to the right side of the hill, then to the left, and cried up to Double Wolf the dreaded words.

"Pony Soldiers! Pony Soldiers——!"

Double Wolf unslung his rifle, as his woman commenced to run with the children through the snow toward the village.

He could not yet see the cavalry, but he was very much afraid. Double Wolf had been at Sand Creek with Black Kettle in that other camp where the Pony Soldiers of Colonel Chivington had come in the early morning shadows. He had lost his first wife and four small children in that terrible time. He knew the same dread that his present woman did. And, in his great fear, he forgot Black Kettle's firm orders not to fire on any soldiers who might come to that camp. He forgot to raise the white cloth and cry out for peace. Instead, he raised his rifle.

When the Pony Soldiers came into his view, he gave a start. The daylight struck the leader of those soldiers.

Double Wolf could see the long curls of red-gold hair cascading beneath the wide black hat. He saw the famous red neckerchief and the high polished boots of that most famous of Pony Soldier chiefs, and he cried out in the Cheyenne tongue, *"Heováe! Heováe!* Yellow Hair! Yellow hair!" And his woman, hearing him, nearly collapsed with fear, and froze in her tracks for a moment. Double Wolf, to protect her, fired directly at Custer. The brave warrior's body was almost cut in two by the answering hail of soldier bullets. Custer did not even look aside as the Indian's bullet whistled harmlessly past him, and Double Wolf died for having fired it. Instead the General calmly raised his hand and signaled the regimental band to commence playing "Garry Owen," the war song of the Seventh Cavalry; and thus it was that the Battle of the Washita was begun.

4. YELLOW HAIR! YELLOW HAIR!

Custer's troopers drove their horses into and across the shallow Washita River. Before them, on the far bank, stood the first of Black Kettle's tipis. The camp was becoming aroused now. Beyond the tipis of the Cheyenne, those of the Arapaho and the Kiowa were stirring. Here and there half-dressed Indians were running out of the warm lodges into the snowy streets of the village, crying out to one another to learn what was wrong. Only the first lodges, those near where Custer now slashed across the icy river, knew that the camp was being attacked by Pony Soldiers. And, as those first few Indians came out into the morning darkness calling and crying out for friends and relatives who might be near, Double Wolf's widow tottered up from the riverbank.

"Yellow Hair! Yellow Hair!" she cried, and the panic of great fear at once swept downward through the entire camp.

Black Kettle, the old chief of peace and friendship for the white brother, stumbled out of his tipi. With him was his wife, also gray-haired and slow of step. They tried to reach some ponies tied nearby, and so escape. The old chief was able to mount a pony, and draw his wife up behind him.

Instantly, the blast of the Pony Soldier carbines struck at the elderly couple.

But the old chief had the heart of a grizzly bear.

He spurred the pony straight at Custer's soldiers, and by a miracle broke through them and drove on for the river.

12

Black Kettle had no rifle—he was not firing at the soldiers. His woman, too, was innocent of weapons. Both wanted only to escape with their lives. But the troopers of the Seventh Cavalry had had their orders, and the carbines roared again.

Down went the laboring pony, shot through a dozen times. Black Kettle never moved when he fell with the pony. His woman struggled to her feet and ran a few more steps. The soldier fire pelted into her back. She twisted about, came back to her mortally wounded husband, fell near him, crawled until she could reach out and touch his hand, then moved no more. The soldiers rushed on, leaping their horses over the silent couple.

After that, the Indian camp had no chance.

Custer had planned the attack too well. Everywhere that the desperate warriors and their families ran, soldiers were there before them. Most of the Indians were unarmed, having had no time to secure weapons, or to load rifles, in the surprise of the dawn assault. Women and children died with the fighting men. A soldier bullet screaming through the half-darkness of the early day could not see what it struck.

Below the camp, the soldiers of Major Elliott cut off the escape. To the south, Colonel Meyers not only blocked escape, but also had seized the entire Cheyenne pony herd, the greatest tragedy which might befall any plains Indian camp. Now all thoughts of flight must be of flight on foot. And who could run so fast as to outdistance a rifle's bullet?

The Indians understood then that they were trapped.

There remained but a single avenue of possible escape, and that was the riverbed of the Washita. If they might reach the stream's low banks of prairie clay, they could fight from behind those banks, as they moved downstream to try and unite with their Arapaho and Kiowa brothers.

Yet, once more, the dreaded Yellow Hair was before them.

He had seen that they must turn for the river. And

across the course of the Washita he had stationed a picked troop of sharpshooters under Lieutenant Billy Cook. When the terrified Cheyenne began running for the banks of the stream, they ran directly into the heavy fire of Cook's hidden sharpshooters.

The fleeing people fell among the rocks of the streambed, or over the steep-cut banks, into the water itself. Their bodies bobbed and floated, or lay half in, half out, of the icy current. Still, by sheer courage, the last of Black Kettle's warriors, a group of some eighty wounded and smoke-blackened braves, reached the shelter of the riverbank and began to fight their way toward the camp of the Arapaho, next down the stream from their own.

The heavy rifle-fire which had been coming from that lower camp now commenced to slacken. Hearing this, Custer threw up his gauntleted hand and shouted for his men to hold their own fire.

"By heaven, boys!" he cried, high voice cracking. "We've got them! That's Elliott slowing his fire down there. The fight's over! He's got them on the run at his end, too!"

But the fight was not over.

The little Osage scout, Hard Rope, rode his pony up to the General. "No quit now," he warned. "Him soldier down there no stop shoot on purpose."

"What?" shouted Custer, grinning through the dust and gunsmoke which still swirled about. "Say what you mean, you red rascal! But be quick. I'm going down there and congratulate Elliott. What a day!"

"You no go down there," said Hard Rope, his wrinkled face suddenly dark with uneasiness. "Me hear Arapaho war-talk down there. Heap more Cheyenne, too. Something bad down there."

By this time California Joe was also growing restless.

"General, something *is* wrong down there. Listen—"

Custer and his officers who had come up to join him in the moment of triumph, all fell still.

"You don't hear a one of our carbines bellowing," said

California Joe, ominously. "They got a deep sound. It booms, sort of. All you hear down there where Major Elliott went are sharp barks. Them's Winchesters talking down yonder, General. Injun guns."

For the first time the flushed face of the Seventh's leader grew pale. A chill not borne in the winter air struck him.

Instantly, the atmosphere shifted from victory to apprehension, as the crowding troops caught the scent of fear.

But Custer was no coward.

"All right," he said quietly. "We must then take a strong force and proceed at once past the big bend to Major Elliott's aid. Recall Captain Cook and form up the troops of Captain Thompson behind my own."

In a very few minutes, the troops were probing toward the increasing stillness beyond the big bend. In another few minutes they had reached the bend and gone beyond it, halfway across a large open meadow toward the camp of the Arapaho. But they went no farther. Suddenly, California Joe, riding beside Custer in the advance, reined in his pony. He seized the General's arm and pointed to the hills which loomed above the river where Elliott's fire had last been heard. The sun was rising, now, just tipping the high ridges to the east, sending its warming light into the meadow.

But Custer was not warmed by what he saw upon those hills.

As far as the eye could reach, on both banks of the Washita, the slopes were covered with warriors from the lower camps. Their weapons glittered in the morning sun. The eagle feathers of their warbonnets flashed everywhere. These were not sleepy old men and squaws and little children routed from warm buffalo robes and running half-naked through the snow. These were full-grown fighting men. And they were dressed for war, and had their rifles and their ammunition belts, and were all watching like a gathering of red wolves the halted command of General Yellow Hair Custer.

"General," said California Joe, "all due respects to you and the Seventh Cavalry, sir, but we'd best get out of here *right now*."

Hard Rope, the Osage, moved his arm in a sweeping circle, all about the meadowland.

"Look him tall grass," he said. "Grass no stop bullet."

Custer was a bulldog of a man. Once he had an idea in his grip, he disliked extremely to let it go. He had started out to find Major Elliott. He was not going to be frightened off by any hillside full of feathered warriors.

"We will go forward," he said. "Bugler, sound the advance!"

The trumpeter raised his horn to obey. But the call never came. As if awaiting a signal, the hundreds upon hundreds of Indians standing silently on the slopes broke into deep and wild war cries. It was a sound to put the fear of death in any white man. And, with it, the painted warriors surged downward, toward the startled troops of the Seventh.

"General," said California Joe, "you had better change that order to the bugle boy. And mighty quicklike, too."

"But what about Elliott?" frowned Custer. "By thunder, man, we can't leave him over there!"

"General," replied the tall scout, tight-lipped, "wherever the major is, over there, or anywhere else, he's past all help of ours. Unless you want your own men to join his, you had best tell that bugler to blow retreat. And right now!"

Custer took one last look across the meadow. The advancing red men were into the tall grass now, weaving through it like a horde of angry ants. The first of their rifle-fire was beginning to patter and pelt like falling rain into the meadow hay about the troopers of the Seventh Cavalry.

"Trumpeter," he said, his pale blue eyes dark with the shadows of shame and doubt, "sound the recall."

5. THE STILLNESS ALONG
   THE WASHITA

Before Custer's troops could get out of the meadow, they were joined by a large number of Major Elliott's men, led by a young lieutenant. This officer said Elliott's troops had killed thirty-eight Cheyenne and taken no great casualties of their own. But when questioned upon the major's whereabouts, the lieutenant showed surprise. He had thought to find Major Elliott with Custer. Where was the major?

No one answered the grim question, and the retreat resumed to the first village.

There Custer began his regrouping. The buglers continued to blow recall, and in response the various troop units began to come in. Before long, of the principal commanders only Major Elliott was still unreported. At this point, Custer believed that his own position was safe enough. He was trying to decide whether to retire from the field with what victory had already been his, or to march on down the river and clean out the Arapaho camp as well. It was in his mind to do the latter, as he would enhance his triumph considerably if he could add the scalp of the Arapaho leader, Big Mouth, to that of the Cheyenne chief, Black Kettle. But at the moment of issuing the order to re-commence the offensive, California Joe and Captain Benteen came up with the Osage scout, Hard Rope, and a captive Arapaho squaw. This woman, who spoke broken English, informed Custer that there were eight hundred lodges scattered along the next five miles of the Washita River and that for the soldiers to advance farther would be to invite a massacre of monstrous proportions.

Custer, of course, said that the woman was lying. She was attempting to stop the renewal of the attack, so that her murderous tribesmen might escape.

But the squaw, with an Indian's dignity, drew her blanket about her. She threw out an arm, pointing dramatically to the hills which surrounded the upper camp, as they did the lower meadow where Elliott had disappeared.

"Look, Yellow Hair!" she cried. "See for yourself. Me no lie. You want lose hair like Oak Leaf Chief?"

"Good Lord, sir!" broke in Captain Benteen. "Oak Leaf Chief is their term for a major's gold shoulder-leaves."

"Yes, yes, you fool," said Custer, irritably. "I know that. Say what you mean, Benteen."

"The woman is trying to tell us that Major Elliott is dead," answered the level-voiced captain. "And she is telling you that you will be the same, if you don't turn about and get out of here while the getting is good."

Custer glared at the other officer. He did not care for Captain Frederick W. Benteen, and the latter believed what he had told the young lieutenant in Custer's tent before the battle: that Yellow Hair actually suffered from delusions of great power, of invincibility, and that the famous long-haired general was not of sound mind.

"Benteen," said Custer now, in a cold voice, "do not interfere again. We will discuss your behavior at a later time."

"I'm certain that we will," said Benteen, returning the commander's angry stare with quiet restraint. "But right now let's discuss the behavior of those Indians gathering across the river."

Quickly, Custer and all the officers saw that the situation of the open meadow was about to be repeated. The number of the braves visible now was beyond hundreds, however. It was California Joe, the chief of the General's scouts, who spoke of this altered fact.

"General, I believe there's somewhat like fifteen hundred—mebbe two thousand—hostiles up there. I further believe they mean to charge us any minute. You've poked a hornet's nest, sir, and they're only beginning to swarm back at you."

Custer, for all his faults of rashness and thoughtlessness, had the mind of a fox. He saw at once that the scout was right. More importantly by far, he understood what he must do about it.

"Captain Meyers," he said calmly, "if your men and the sharpshooters of Lieutenant Cook will kindly keep those Indians away from us for half an hour, we shall be all finished here. Please commence firing at once, sir."

So it was that, under the protection of the best riflemen in the Seventh Cavalry, Yellow Hair set about the final destruction of Black Kettle's camp.

His treacherous attack on the Cheyenne village had brought him sixty captured squaws with their surviving children. On the icy ground about the lodges lay the bodies of the Indian dead. One hundred three warrors. Sixteen women. Eleven small children. Piled high between the lodges were the articles of triumph: 241 saddles . . . 1123 tanned buffalo hides . . . 82 rifles and revolvers . . . 425 axes and lances . . . 4035 arrows and warbows . . . 2185 blankets . . . 535 pounds of gunpowder . . . 1375 pounds of lead and bullets . . . 700 pounds of tobacco . . . Untold thousands of pounds of buffalo meat cured for the winter.

All of this plunder was now piled in one enormous heap.

To this vast pile were added all of the tipis, pulled over by ropes and dragged in by the troopers on their horses.

Over the now mountainous pyramid of Indian life-goods, the more than five hundred pounds of gunpowder were sprinkled.

"Stand away, men!" shouted Custer. Then, high-voiced to his waiting orderly, "You may go ahead, sir. Fire it."

The orderly, standing by with a burning brand seized from one of the Cheyenne tipi fires, hurled the flaming torch into the pile. There was a single moment's pause, then a belching roar of fire leaped upward, and the black smoke began to roll across the Washita. Custer, as calmly as though standing on the parade ground at Fort Wallace, turned to his scouts.

"Hard Rope," he said, "have your Osage braves bring over the captured ponies. Drive them out into the open by the river, where those Indians across the stream may see them."

"What are you going to do, General?" asked Benteen.

"I am thinking of an old Cheyenne proverb," responded Custer. "Kill an Indian of the plains, and two more will spring up to take his place; but destroy that Indian's pony, and his heart for war drops dead within him."

And so it was.

The Osage brought forward the beautiful herd of Black Kettle's people. The rifles of Lieutenant Cook's sharpshooters commenced to roar out their deep bellowing reports. Some say that it lasted for one hour. Some say much less, even so little as the thirty minutes Custer had promised.

But the result was the same, by either time.

When the last Pony Soldier carbine had boomed out, eight hundred seventy-five Cheyenne horses lay dead or dying upon the banks of the Washita. And Yellow Hair's proverb had come true.

Across the stream, the rifles of the horrified Cheyenne had been stilled for many minutes. The warriors could not fight while their beloved ponies were being destroyed. They withdrew upon the hills in silent hundreds. Then, without another sound, their entire number—California Joe always maintained there were three thousand of them—rode slowly from that terrible field. They went away down the river. No single further shot was fired by either side. No war whoop rang. No bugles blew. The troopers were as stunned, almost, as the broken-hearted Indians.

As quietly as the departing Cheyenne, Custer marshaled his Seventh Cavalry and left the field.

He went westward, back along his own tracks through the snow, abandoning brave Major Elliott and all other men not reported by that time. Behind him he left only the smoke and the drift of the ashes and the smell of death in the lovely Valley of the Washita.

That and the terrible silence.

The Cheyenne never forgot him, and they never forgave him. They vowed, as they rode away through that stillness on the Washita, that some day, along some distant trail, they would meet again with Yellow Hair beside another river.

PART TWO

THE PA SAPA

6.   RED CLOUD'S TREATY

The snows of two winters had fallen. It was 1870, and
the Indians of the South Plains were quiet, their spirits
defeated by Custer. For the most part there was peace.
And for the most part the Cheyenne and the Arapaho
obeyed their Medicine Lodge Treaty with the white
man, staying on or near their reservations below the
Arkansas. There was good reason they should. The
buffalo were extremely fat that year, and there were a
great many of them. Also, the treaty to which their
chiefs had touched the pen at Medicine Lodge Creek
—at about the same time the Sioux and the Cheyenne of
the North were signing the Laramie Treaty of 1868
—that treaty promised the Indian that no white man
might come south of the Arkansas River to hunt the
buffalo, or any of the other of the Indians' game animals.
So there was peace in the South, as in the North, and the
white people across the land began to hope that the
bloody wars with the red men were a thing of the
frontier past.

They hoped far too soon.

In the North the great Red Cloud was preparing to
travel to Washington, the mighty village of the Great
Father. The Sioux leader rode to the east upon the Iron
Horse, the white man's railroad. He saw in the great city
of Washington all of the wonders of the white man. He
realized how many of the enemy there were. He saw
their huge cannon. He saw all of their thousands of
soldiers, both Walkaheaps of the Infantry and Pony
Soldiers of the Cavalry. Red Cloud was an intelligent

man. His eyes told him that the Indians could no longer fight the white man. But his heart was heavy, all the same, and there was a reason for that.

His people had told him that he must find out from the Great Father in Washington exactly what that fine treaty of 1868 had said. Many chiefs of the Sioux and the northern Cheyenne, and of the Arapaho, said that the treaty had promised the red man that, "so long as the grass shall grow," no white man would come into their lands, neither to travel through them, nor to hunt within them, nor to build or camp or settle in any way upon them. Yet the road of the Iron Horse had been built where it frightened away the buffalo. The wagons of the settlers going west still camped in Indian country, still chopped down Indian trees, grazed out Indian pastures. And now, most unhappy thing of all, even the beautiful Black Hills, the sacred *Pa Sapa* of the Sioux, were being violated by white hunters and wanderers. Such things were wrong.

So it was that when his trip was nearly at an end, and he was to be put once more upon the Iron Horse, Red Cloud spoke to the great chiefs in Washington, saying that he and his people must hear, at last, exactly the true tongue of the New Laramie Treaty.

The Secretary of the Interior, a good man and one who had some understanding of the simple, childlike faith of the Indian mind, had the treaty brought forward and translated, word-by-word, for the proud and haughty leader of the Sioux.

For the first time in his life, Red Cloud was brought to understand what he had done; was made to see what he had signed away for his people when he touched the pen for them.

There were three main things:

The treaty declared that the Indians agreed to leave forever their wild free life hunting the buffalo and the elk and the fleet antelope, and to settle down upon small fenced places and to become peaceful farmers like their white brothers who would soon come and plow up the buffalo pastures.

The treaty stated that the Indians would peacefully permit the building of railroads—as many as the white man wished—across the buffalo ranges, and that they would not attack the Iron Horse, nor tear up its steel rails, nor bring down any of its telegraph wires, but stay far away and do nothing.

And in its last, most secret term, the treaty said that the Indians promised to retire to, and never to stray again away from, the new reservations prepared for them in the barren and gameless lands far eastward of their high plains homes, hard against the banks of the *Mini Sosi*, the Big Muddy River, the Missouri.

Red Cloud had no guile to match that of the white man. He was brave and he had pride as fierce as that of the wild horse. It is said that, when the interpreters had told him these things which he had promised in the name of his people, the prairie chieftain uttered a great cry and leaped to his feet. As swiftly, he drew from within his blanket a pistol which he had carried there, unknown to any, all of those days. He put the muzzle of the weapon to his temple and would have killed himself, except that some of his fellow chiefs sprang upon him and took the gun away from him.

But, even so, his wild heart was broken.

He said that he would treat no more with the white brother. He said that he would go home and tell his people of the shame which he had brought upon them.

"But I will tell them," he cried, drawing himself to his full height, and his voice growling like summer thunder far across the plains, "that they must not believe this treaty! I will say to them, 'Come, my brothers. We are few and the white man is as many as the heads of the grass. But let us fight him so long as our ponies live to bear us forward, and let us keep on fighting him. He has lied and made fools of us. He has made a fool and a liar of me. There can be no peace with liars.'"

Here the angry chief paused. His muscular arm shot outward, menacing all of the Peace Commissioners.

"From this day," he said, "stay away from my people——!"

The good-hearted Secretary, and the well-meaning members of the Peace Commission—all of the Indians' friends who were present—made haste to quiet the chief's anger.

But in other parts of the nation's capital, the reaction was not so kindly.

Said crusty President Grant when informed of the uproar over Red Cloud's impassioned outcry:

"Nonsense; tell that Indian to go home and start plowing."

7. THAT THIEVES' ROAD

But the Indian Bureau would not take Grant's hard-headed advice. Its members persuaded Red Cloud not to go home, but to go to New York City and make one more plea for "understanding," one more appeal for "peace and brotherhood."

This time the Sioux chief had a far larger audience.

His speech was carried in all of the large metropolitan newspapers. It was picked up by the smaller papers and spread across the land. Red Cloud rose to soaring heights of Indian eloquence in stating the case for his wronged people. At no point did he mention the scores of white women and children killed or kidnaped by his savage warriors of the Oglala, Hunkpapa, Minniconjou, Brulé, Yankton and Sans Arc bands of the Dakota Sioux. Or, if he did admit these tragedies, the fact failed to reach his listeners through the lips of the Indian Bureau interpreters.

All that the American people understood was that here was a brave and noble red man who had been robbed and betrayed by the "white devils," and made to sacrifice his own people by signing the "notorious treaty" of 1868.

Public indignation was instant. The Secretary of the Interior was forced to alter the reservation clause. The Sioux, henceforth, would be free to "trade as they wished." This new triumph of the peace party meant one thing alone in Indian terms. From that time forward, the Sioux could come and go as they wished. The new "treaty" was nothing less than a guarantee that they

28

could return to their old warlike way of life, riding and raiding where they wished, so long as they called it "trade." Red Cloud went back to his western home, not to plow, but to put on the war paint.

For the next three years, and into the fourth summer, that of 1874, the Sioux plundered and burned and scalped from the Dakotas down into Kansas, and westward from the Missouri River into the mining country of Colorado and far Montana. No settler, no prospector, no wagon party was safe. The north plains were "made bloody" by the Sioux, as the south plains had been ravaged in the years before by the Cheyenne and the Arapoho, the Comanche and the Kiowa. Nowhere on the frontier was this more true than in Red Cloud's own homeland of the Black Hills. Here, his fierce Oglala tribesmen, under such famed chiefs as Crazy Horse and American Horse, would not listen to anything but war.

Oh, they had a peace chief and a white-talker of their own, even as the Cheyenne had had in old Black Kettle.

The Sioux friend of the white man was named Spotted Tail, and he was old and wise and had been to Washington before Red Cloud. Spotted Tail prayed and pleaded that his people would listen to him in time.

"Hear the Great Father," he warned. "Obey his words. If he tells you to go home and farm the land, do that. For I have been to his great village in the East. We cannot fight all those people. Believe what I say. Obey your Father who lives in Washington!"

But the Sioux would far rather hear what Tashunka Witko or Nakpa Kesela had to say; they much preferred to listen to Crazy Horse and American Horse.

"Cover your ears!" these fighters cried. "Do not hear the old man! The white men have bought his tongue and they have split it in the middle like the tongue of a snake, and it speaks in two different directions at the same time. Ride with us. Stay free. Do not let the white men lie to you again. This land is ours! Are you all old women, that you will no longer fight for what is yours?"

So it came about that the peace party in the Indian

Bureau brought woe and distress to the very people they intended to protect.

The public lost sympathy for Red Cloud's folk.

The newspapers and the politicians began to demand some action by the Government to stop the raiding and the pillaging of "innocent settlers and honest husband-men."

Now it was the turn of the war party in Washington.

An expedition, it was announced, would be mounted at once. Its purpose would be to "explore" the Black Hills—the very heart of the Sioux country—seeking to establish a wagon road through them, and to find a location for the building of an army fort which would "threaten" the warlike spirits of the "spoiled red children" throughout the length and breadth of their sacred Land of the Spotted Eagle.

This expedition was to have results so dark as to be beyond imagination at the moment. Wise heads, both red and white, understood this and tried in vain to stop any such foolhardy invasion of the treatylands which the government had guaranteed in writing to the red man "for as long as the grass shall grow."

It was no use.

Across the United States a hard depression had set in. Times were very bad. The public could see no sense, at all, in continuing to spend millions of dollars to pacify the Sioux when white children were going hungry, and white fathers could find no work, and white mothers toiled long hours merely to put a scrap of food on the table. Suddenly, the people had had their fill of the false propaganda of the Indian Peace Party. Let Red Cloud look out for himself! So far as the temper of the times was concerned, he and his folk would not get another dime of what was now openly being called "blackmail" to stay peaceful. Let the Indians feed themselves for a change. "Uncle Sam's children" were tired of taking care of their red brothers and sisters.

As for the response of the Sioux to this hardening attitude, it was too late for helpful change.

The red man never had understood the peace policy which sought to buy his friendship with food and gifts. In his view, such generosity was a sign of weakness and fear. The more he was given, the more he demanded, and the more he came to believe that the Americans were soft and cowardly.

Thinking this, he made the mistake of his red life.

The War Department moved swiftly ahead with its plan to invade the last sanctuary of the plains Indian, to drive a wagon trail through the Black Hills, a trail that the Sioux would forever after call "That Thieves' Road."

The department selected for the commander of this fateful expedition the most dangerous of all possible soldier chiefs for the purpose.

He was a man the Indians remembered.

Indeed, he was a man they had sworn never to forget, or to forgive.

His name was General George Armstrong Custer.

8. GOLD IN THE BLACK HILLS!

Fort Abraham Lincoln stood across the Missouri River from Bismarck, North Dakota. Custer had been named its commander in the winter of 1873, before the fort was finished. Now, in the spring of 1874, the new post was completed. The Seventh Cavalry had moved into its prairie home and Custer had returned from a journey eastward to fetch his lovely young wife, Elizabeth, to the far Dakotas to share his lonely command.

That spring was surely one of the happiest in the young general's life.

But the excitement which stirred him was not brought by "Libbie" Custer, alone.

Yellow Hair was high in spirit because soon he would be gone again into the Indian Country. Soon he and the Seventh Cavalry would be back in the saddle, riding out there where the Sioux warriors waited, faces smeared with black and yellow paint, fierce eyes watching for him who was only truly happy when the feathered bonnets were flashing far off, the trumpeter blowing the charge, the gray and the black and the bay horses of the Seventh Cavalry thundering into the chase. Ah! if he could but get one good fight from the red rascals this time!

He well recalled the past summer, when he had ridden up and down the Yellowstone River with General Stanley looking for some Sioux to defeat. The thought of it made his face flush. Not only had he not found the Sioux, but the Sioux had found him. Two separate times. And not only had he not defeated the red horsemen, but they had beaten him badly on both occasions. The

second time Custer's command had barely been saved
from a massacre by the timely arrival of General Stanley
with the infantry troops. Moreover, Yellow Hair had
suffered the added humiliation of being put under arrest
by Stanley for disobeying orders!

Custer remembered something else about that Yellowstone march of 1873. That was the name of the
Indian who had so nearly caught him and killed him. It
was the famed Sioux chieftain, Rain-in-the-Face. How
could he forget that Indian? Rain-in-the-Face had killed
his two good friends, Doctor Holzinger, the veterinary
of the Seventh Cavalry, and Balarian, the popular post
sutler at Fort Lincoln, in the first scrape with the chief's
Sioux war party.

Now, if Custer's luck would bring him another chance
to meet that treacherous savage, things would be different! In fact, just let any of the Sioux try an thing with
the Black Hills column. Yellow Hair would show them.
Those Indians needed a lesson. And the Seventh Cavalry
were just the boys who could give it to them.

Forward, ho——!

The long line of troops and supply vehicles rolled out
of Fort Abraham Lincoln on the second of June, 1874.

With Custer were ten troops of cavalry, the regimental band, two companies of infantry, one hundred
wagons, three Gatling guns and a three-inch cannon, a
herd of beef cattle to feed the soldiers, a corps of
newspaper reporters, photographers and assorted guests
from the East who had simply been invited along "for the
sport" by the good-natured, high-strung commander of
the Seventh Cavalry.

Custer well understood the need for letting the
outside world know about his daring exploits and adven-
tures.

Hence, the people of the press, and the cameramen.

Some of Yellow Hair's officers, the sober and older
ones like Captain Benteen and Major Marcus Reno, said
that the "Boy General" scarcely went to shave in the

mornings but that he alerted the reporters to come along and see if he might cut himself.

But every great man has his critics.

Custer was so popular with the American public that even President Grant, who intensely disliked him, was forced to tender favors to the long-haired "hero of the Washita." Indeed, Grant had at first refused to even let Custer accompany the Black Hills Expedition, far from commanding it. But kind old General Terry and peppery Phil Sheridan had begged Grant to relent, and the tough old Civil War commander had given in against his better judgment.

"He is a vain fool," the blunt, cigar-chomping President was said to have growled in private. "And not one-half the soldier those blasted reporters are forever saying."

Custer could not have cared less had he heard the remark.

He had his command, the old Seventh, again at his back. Out toward the sunset, where the troops were heading, the Sioux waited. Now they would see how Yellow Hair repaid his debts. Now that haughty Red Cloud and that traitorous Rain-in-the-Face would get what was coming to them.

But the long days passed, the column wound onward and onward, and in all of the time not a single eagle-feather bonnet was spied from afar, not a solitary Indian ponytrack was seen by the eager scouts of the Seventh Cavalry.

At last, after nearly three weeks, the Black Hills rose along the southwestern horizon. The land commenced immediately to grow more fair with each mile. Soon the trroops were winding into the beautiful hills themselves, and their wondering eyes were seeing for the first time why the wild and savage red horsemen of the plains called these places "sacred."

Custer, always a man with a quick and sensitive eye for loveliness, be it in nature or in the slender graces of a young woman, could not contain his spirits.

"There is such grazing here," he said, "that its only fault can be that it is too luxuriant!" He found, also, "crystal streams of water so cold as to render ice undesirable even at noontime."

Tall grass and flowers grew to the knees of the riding troopers. Pine trees dotted the lovely meadows. Lakes and streams were everywhere. High clouds drifted in a sky "blue as angel's eyes." The air was soft and brilliant with sunshine, yet deliciously cool after the parching heat of the level plain which surrounded the Sioux paradise.

"I know of no portion of our great nation," rhapsodized the General, "where nature has done so much to prepare homes for the husbandmen and left so little for the latter to do as here. Nowhere in the States have I tasted cultivated berries of better flavor than those found growing wild here. Cattle could winter in these valleys without other food or shelter than that to be obtained from running at large."

But Custer was only getting started.

On top of all these unbelievable bounties of nature which had been discovered in the Black Hills, there was another gift of value positively staggering.

"*Gold*," proclaimed the reports sifting back to civilization from the leader of the Seventh Cavalry, "*is to be found at the very grassroots.*"

The first response to this was a thin trickle of men who were near the scene, rugged and tough westerners who had only to turn their pack mules toward the Dakotas to be "on their way." The real flood came when Custer, after sixty days away in the field, returned to Fort Lincoln to begin writing up his "magnificent exploration" for the magazines and newspapers of the country.

With that, the rush was on.

Hundreds upon hundreds of greedy whites poured into the sacred Hills in search of what the astonished Indians called "the useless yellow metal." The situation became ugly almost at once. By the early autumn the Government knew that, unless it took some drastic step, an Indian war would break over the *Pa Sapa* which would make the Washita and Palo Duro and Adobe Wells fights of the southern tribes seem as skirmishes. In a desperate move, Red Cloud was once more called to take the Iron Horse for Washington.

The proud chief, to save his people, consented to try this final time to make an honorable peace.

What awaited him in Washington stunned the Sioux.

It was this, no more and no less:

The Great Father had decided to buy the *Pa Sapa* from the Indians. All that Red Cloud might do for his people was to agree on a fair and fitting price for their beloved Black Hills. No, it was worse than that. All that the Sioux chief might do was to *accept* that price which the Great Father would *tell him* was fitting and fair!

Red Cloud looked at the Indian Commissioners, and could not speak.

What was there to say?

The white men had once more caught him in a *wickmunke*, a trap, and words would never again open its jaws.

Red Cloud knew it, every white man there knew it.

When the springtime came again, and the ponies were fat and strong with the new grass, there would be war.

9. WHAT CUSTER SAW FAR OFF

Autumn deepened in the land of the Dakotas. The short curl of the buffalo grass turned blue-brown, its winter color. The first ice storms, the beginning flurries of small-flaked snows drove across the naked prairies. The Sioux looked up at the leaden skies, listened to the last thin cries of the departing geese, high above the storm.

"*Wasiya* is coming," they said.

Wasiya was the Winter Giant, the Blizzard King.

When he commenced to blow in earnest, to bring the great drift-snows, then Mother Earth went to sleep. The animals sought their dens. The Indians gathered into their winter camps, pitching their snug buffaloskin tipis close together in some sheltered spot, where the people might help one another through the Time of the Big Cold.

And, for this time, the red brother was quiet.

The white brother, too, must bow to the fierce blasts of Wasiya's sub-zero breath. Even he must stay in his lodge and keep warm. His Iron Horses, his Talking Wires of the telegraph, his diggers of the yellow metal, his breakers of the Mother Earth, his Pony Soldiers and his Walkaheap Soldiers—all were forced by Wasiya to lie up and be at peace, even as the Indian.

And so, for a little while, the life was good.

But across the Big Muddy River, at Fort Abraham Lincoln, Yellow Hair Custer grew restless. He was bored with the games and charades, the costume balls and dramatic plays which made up the social life of an isolated far western army post in mid-winter. The minuets, waltzes and Virginia reels supplied by the regimental band were fun at first. Then the musicales performed on the grand piano freighted by army wagon for Libbie all the way from St. Paul relieved the monotony of post life briefly.

But dance balls and piano recitals were scarcely fit substitutes for summer campaigning.

Not for the General.

In truth, "Armstrong," as his adoring wife and close personal friends called him, loved a party and the gay-bright smile of a fair maid as well as any man alive. Yet that winter at Fort Lincoln seemed without end to Custer.

Something, he could not say what, lay in his mind and would not leave it. When his young wife or his officers would question him, he would deny that it was anything; he was the happiest man in the world, he would insist, as what reasonable man would not be with Custer's luck?

But once, when his brother Tom found him deep in brooding thought, he sighed and looked far away toward the southwest and the sacred *Pa Sapa*, the distant Black Hills of Red Cloud and his betrayed people.

"Tom," he said, "if I were an Indian, I would greatly prefer to cast my lot among those of my people who adhered to the free open plains rather than submit to the confined limits of a reservation."

"That's a strange thing for you to say, Autie." Autie was Custer's boyhood nickname, and he did not hear it much these days. But Tom and he were always very close, and the Custers were sentimental people. "You've always been on the other side, I would think," Tom continued. "Why this sudden sadness for the noble red man?"

Tom was not like Custer. He was a bigger man, and much less keen of mind. He was also a heavy drinker, whereas Custer never touched a drop of anything stronger than the clean sparkling water of the mountains and prairies he loved so much. Perhaps this crudeness of the younger brother was what drew the General to

protect and cherish him. In any event, young Tom
Custer was his favorite chick, and the dashing leader of
the Seventh Cavalry mother-henned him on every campaign and in every camp they shared together.

"Well, boy," he now told Tom, "a man is not always
what he seems, is he? Not even to his little brother."

Tom wanted at once to know what that meant, since
he knew Custer did not always say what, precisely, he
had in mind.

"I mean," the General answered him, "that I think the
wild Indian of the American plains has led the finest and
noblest life of any man in history. He drinks the cold
wind, he is wrapped in the warm sun. He is brave, loyal,
generous. He lacks nothing that I admire, or would not
give my all, in another life, to share with him."

Tom frowned. "Are you saying that you wish you had
been born an Indian!?" Tom's frown changed to a grin, as
the absurdity of the thought hit him. "Hah! hah!" he
laughed, big hand slapping his thigh. "Oh, that's rich,
Autie! *You*, an Indian! Ho! ho! ho!"

Custer shook his head.

"Be serious a moment, Tom," he said. "I want to tell
you something."

There was that ring of iron in Cutster's voice which
men did not ignore. He was giving an order to young
Lieutenant Tom Custer, and the latter nodded and sat
down and waited.

Custer's voice softened at once, and he began to talk.

He asked Tom to look around the room. Did he notice
all the stuffed birds and animals staring at them from
every wall and corner? Did he not remember these were
all shot, and many of them mounted, by his famous older
brother? Well, suddenly, all of such youthful fancies as
stuffing animals seemed foolish. Custer was not even
greatly heartened by the recent publication of his first
book, *My Life on the Plains*, in which he told of the
hunting and taking of all those stuffed birds and beasts
which stared at him so remorsefully now.

Did Tom know, yet, how it felt to realize, overnight,

that boyhood and youth were over? That life had fled, like a thief in the dark, and left only middle age behind it? Did he understand that his great hero, the "Boy General," was a boy no longer?

Custer paused here to stride over and stand in front of Tom. He was smiling his old peg-toothed smile, but there was a plaintive quality to it.

"My dear little brother," he said, "look at me; I am thirty-five years old this winter!"

Tom shrugged. "You don't look any different to me, Autie," he said loyally.

"True," nodded Custer. "And to you I never will look any different. Thank you, Tom. But I know I grow old."

"What?" Tom cried. "At thirty-five? Custer, old? Hah!"

But the General was right, and Tom Custer had not the eyes to see it.

Custer's features were taking on the skully look of advancing time. His long nose seemed longer and sharper. His forehead glistened where the hairline had receded. His brows jutted out in a shelf over his pale eyes. His mustache seemed run to weed, flowing to cover his mouth and make his chin appear less resolute and bold. Beyond all, the famed yellow hair had thinned alarmingly. It was still glossy and of full curl behind the ears. But on top he was now combing long strands sideways to cover the growing baldness, and in the rear the legendary curls of "sunbright gold" did not now reach the collar, let alone fall almost to the epaulets, as in the glory days of the Civil War, or the Washita.

"Yes, brother," said Custer now, after long delay. "Old at thirty-five; and if you will bear with me, perhaps you will learn why."

Strangely—or so it seemed to young Tom Custer—the General returned now to his sad-voiced, gentle praise of the plains Indian. There was a spell, almost, in the way that he spoke. Even Tom Custer, that rough-roisterous fellow whose own opinions of the red brother were not fit to mention in polite company, felt the power and the sorrow of his brother's words.

The Indian, Custer began, was in many ways the most admirable of men. Kind to the old and the afflicted, gentle with the lost of mind, loyal to friend, devoted to all children, honoring the given word, punishing the broken vow, he was a man who did not understand the forked tongue of his white brother, and who believed until far too late that simple justice and the fundamental rights of humanity would prevail, preserving both life and liberty.

When at last he saw that this was not true, and that he must fight or die in the bondage of some reservation, the Indian had chosen his way with all of the dignity and pride which were the birthrights of his freedom.

If it was a harsh way that he had chosen, Custer continued, it was also a noble way. And it was necessary.

For there was now no time remaining to the Indian.

There was scarcely time for him to oil his rifle, run in his war pony, make his medicine prayers, say the sacred words to *Wakan Tanka*, his Great Spirit.

For the white man was demanding war or peace. And the peace could be had only at the price of slavery. For the red man, the latter course had become impossible. He knew that where freedom fell unfought for, there men died as if by their own hands. And for him, the Indian, his liberty was the same thing as his life.

Hence, when the white man insisted that the Indian go and stay upon a reservation, forsaking his freedom, the white man was condemning the Indian to death.

"That," said Custer, with a heavy sigh, "is why I am feeling old today, Tom, and not at all like a hero."

Tom Custer was not so crude as to fail to realize he had just heard a genuine eulogy. His older brother did actually admire the savage red horsemen of the plains. But neither was the young lieutenant to be touched by such tributes.

"Autie," he said, bounding to his feet with a laugh, "there's nothing wrong with you that a few weeks out trailing old Rain-in-the-Face won't cure! Come on, General, admit it, now. You'd rather fight redskins than eat!"

Custer looked past him, his glance once more seeking the western window of his study.

"No, Tom," he said, "you're wrong. It won't ever be the same again. Not after this spring. By that time the country will have realized that the Sioux will not sell the *Pa Sapa*."

He paused, going to his desk and picking up a many-paged document. He found the section that he wanted, turned again to Tom. "Let me read you something," he said.

". . . The United States hereby agrees and stipulates that the country north of the North Platte River and east of the summits of the Big Horn Mountains shall be held and considered to be unceded Indian territory, and also stipulates and agrees that no white person or persons shall be permitted to settle upon or occupy any portion of the same; or without the consent of the Indians first had and obtained, to pass through same; and it is further agreed by the United States that within ninety days after the conclusion of peace with all the bands of the Sioux nation, the military posts now established in the territory of this article named shall be abandoned, and that the road leading to them and by them to the Territory of Montana shall be closed . . ."

Custer returned the paper to his desk.

"That," he said to Tom, "is Article 16 of the Treaty of 1868, signed at Fort Rice with the Sioux and allied tribes. *That* is what we promised them. But what we are giving them, when this new spring comes, will be the greatest horde of white rascals that ever invaded any land. When our people understand that their Government is going to buy that land from the Indians, and the Indians be damned, there will be utterly no stopping the rush for mineral and ranching rights in the Black Hills.

And I, Tom, your own brother—I was the one who opened up that Pandora's box for the poor devils."

"Oh, nonsense!" said the irrepressible Tom. "Somebody had to do it."

"Wait," said Custer. "There's more."

He picked up a second document from his littered desk. Waving it briefly, he tossed it back among the other papers.

"Instructions just in from the War Department," he said. "When the big rush starts this spring, the Seventh Cavalry is ordered to stand by and watch. We are not to interfere, Tom, neither on the Indian side, nor on that of the whites. Do you understand what that is going to mean?"

"I can't say that I do, General," smiled Tom. "But then I never was any threat to the bright boys in the class!"

"It means, sir," said Custer, speaking with deadly seriousness, "the end of the Indians."

"Well!" cried Tom, relieved, not sensing, either, his brother's foreboding mood. "Good riddance to them, sir, and the sooner the quicker. Where's your tragedy in that?"

Custer did not answer him.

Instead he turned back to the window.

He stood there long after Tom Custer had left, staring into the winter sunset, a far-off light in his pale eyes.

Was he seeing into that future which awaited him along the sunlit banks of that other river where the tongueless dead of the Washita had promised to wait for him?

PART THREE

POWDER RIVER

10. THE VISION DREAMER— TATANKA YOTANKA

There followed, in that year of 1875, a period of strange quiet in the Land of the Spotted Eagle. From Fort Abraham Lincoln to far Montana and Wyoming, wherever the Sioux held sway, there were no major conflicts between white man and red.

The spring which Custer had feared would bring the showdown brought instead only puzzled reports from his scouts as to a peculiar scarcity of Indians.

Could it be because the buffalo herds had moved farther west? Were the Sioux merely following their food supply?

It was true that, with the coming of the new grass, a brawling flood of white goldhunters and homeseekers had struck the Black Hills. In this, the General had been precisely correct. But the Indians, instead of fighting the white invaders to the death, as both the army and the Indian Bureau had been so certain they would, seemed to have left the country with the buffalo and other wild game ahead of the renewed invasion of the hated "pale-eyes."

Might the do-gooders of the Peace Policy group have been right all along?

Was filling his savage stomach more important to the red man, after all, than defending his supposedly sacred lands and liberty?

Much white opinion now came to believe this. Newspapers proclaimed it. The Sioux were "getting out." They had just simply "run off and hid." They would "never stand and fight now." "The so-called 'Indian Wars' in the west," trumpeted one famed journal, "are as good as over."

But the country and the newspapers were wrong.

Far out across the plains of Montana and Wyoming, where the Powder River and the Tongue and the Rosebud and the Big Horn flowed, the Sons of the Spotted Eagle were gathering. The strange quiet and the peculiar scarcity of the Sioux in the sacred lands of the *Pa Sapa* were not things of accident. Nor were they evidences of surrender. The truth lay many long pony journeys from any such foolish white man's boastings as these.

For the Sioux had found a new leader.

He was a man who had risen steadily and with supreme use of talk to a position of power within their nation.

He was not a war chief, not a fighting man, but a leader of the people. In the ways of the nomad red horsemen of the high plains, in their names for such things, he would be called a medicine man. He was not tall and handsome like Red Cloud. He was not a great orator like Spotted Tail. Nor was he a hero to the Sioux such as the famed Crazy Horse. He was, in fact, a short and homely man of middle years. He wore no dazzling burst of eagle feathers in his warbonnet, but only a solitary black feather slanted through the long braid of his dark hair. Yet his was greater power than that of any war chief, for he could see into the future—his eyes were the eyes of a vision-dreamer, and the Sioux of all the seven bands gathered to him.

This man was of the Hunkpapa tribe, with the Oglala of Crazy Horse the fiercest of all the Sioux peoples.

The vision which he proclaimed was one which aroused the red heart, stirred the Sioux blood, called to the Indian pride of all the tribes—the Cheyenne and the Arapaho most importantly—to rise up and stand tall with their Sioux brothers in one last great war upon the white man.

The name of this man was Tatanka Yotanka.

But that is not the name by which the white men called him, and by which history was to remember him.

His other name was the one which came to turn the white man's blood cold.

It was Sitting Bull.

11. THE DECISION OF CRAZY HORSE

It was a beautiful autumn. The buffalo were sleek and fat. Their great curly coats were deepening for the winter. The September and October moons went quickly. The hunting was good. Well before the first moon of the Big Cold, December, the lodges of the Sioux were filled with a fine supply of buffalo meat. Many glossy hides had been tanned and made into warm sleeping-robes for the snug tipis. The buffalo—the Indians called him "Uncle Pte"—had , as always, supplied both food and bed to the red man. *Ha-a-u! Ha-a-u!*

Spirits rose. Thanks were offered to Wakan Tanka, the Great Spirit.

It was true that the Cheyenne and the Arapaho had not yet joined in Sitting Bull's plan for a last great battle against the whites. But neither had they rejected the idea. They were thinking it over, they said. They would make up their minds in the springtime. That was the time for war, anyway.

Who made war in the wintertime?

Sitting Bull was not angry. He was sad. What did it take, he asked the Cheyenne, for them to realize that they must fight the white man? Why did they not understand, by this time, that the white man broke all of his treaties? That he lied about everything?

Did not the Cheyenne remember what had happened to Makhpiya Luta, to Red Cloud, only the autumn before this one? How the white man had called him again to Washington and told him that they were going to buy the Black Hills then and there? How they had set a price upon the *Pa Sapa*, and Red Cloud and his people could either pay it, or get out?

Did not the Cheyenne remember that price?

Did they not remember the Indian Commission coming out to Red Cloud's country with its offers, when the Sioux chief had stormed out of Washington in rightful anger?

Let Sitting Bull remind them, then. That price was only $6,000,000 for outright purchase, or $400,000 per year for the right of the white man to hunt gold wherever he pleased in the *Pa Sapa*. Was not that a sorrowful enough thing for the Cheyenne to remember? Were they not stirred by Red Cloud's answer? Had they forgotten that, also?

Listen, then:

"I will not even consider such a price," Makhpiya told the white chiefs. "I demand a hundred times your amount, and moreover the Government must support the Sioux for seven generations to come. The Government has brought my people from their hunting grounds and made them to live upon their reservations like white men. It is only reasonable, then, that the white man shall pay all of the expenses and supply all of the needs of the Indian."

And did not the Cheyenne brothers of the Sioux recall also what followed, the saddest thing of all? How the white man had said to Red Cloud, "If you do not go home and do as you are told, coming onto the reservation and staying there, all rations will be withheld from your people until you consent." And how the once proud and haughty Red Cloud had surrendered to this wicked threat, and gone home and told his people he could fight no more for them. How he had said he could not see them starve, could not look into the faces of the women and the old people and the children asking him for food, and that they must then, all of them, do as the white man said, and go and live upon the reservation.

Were the Cheyenne going to let this same evil shame be brought upon their own people?

Or would they not, at last, come to their senses and join with Sitting Bull and Crazy Horse?

Was it not better, in the end, to die as men than to live as old women and cowards?

So spoke the vision-dreamer of the fierce Hunkpapa.

But the Cheyenne still said that they were not sure. It was a terrible decision to make. Give them yet a little more time. Perhaps the white man would relent. Perhaps he would show some gentleness and charity in his heart, after all, and let those Indians who were still free, stay free.

Did he not have most of the Indians already on the reservations, suggested Two Moons, the Cheyenne chief.

Of course he did.

Down in the south plains, the Cheyenne and the Comanche, the Kiowa and the Arapaho, were all coming in now.

The war down there was all over.

Perhaps it was all over up in the north, too. Did not Sitting Bull see this possible good thing? Why make war plans when peace might still be in the hearts of the white man? Wait until the spring, anyway. Then decide.

There was nothing that Sitting Bull or Crazy Horse could do about this Cheyenne refusal to fight, or to face reality.

And, silently, they despaired of support from their Cheyenne brothers—support which the Sioux must have, to win.

But where their own red kin could not convince the warriors of Two Moons, the white man would try.

And he did.

Upon the third day of December, 1875, a fateful letter sped from the Secretary of the Interior to the Indian Bureau. Its contents were secret, but they soon leaked out.

This is what the letter said:

. . . Referring to our communications of the 27th
ultimo, relative to the status of certain Sioux Indians
residing without the bounds of their reservation and
their continued hostile attitude toward the whites, I
have to request that you direct the Indian Agents at
all Sioux agencies in Dakota and at Fort Peck,
Montana, to notify said Indians that unless they shall
remove within the bounds of their reservation and
remain there, before the 31st of January next, they
shall be deemed hostile and treated accordingly by
the military . . .

Now it was to be seen that the white man, too, had a
plan for war. But his plan would not wait for spring, or
for the Cheyenne. His plan was already under way.

It was in the coldest part of the winter. The camps of
Sitting Bull and of Crazy Horse (the "certain Sioux" and
"said Indians" referred to in the Secretary's secret order)
were far, far from the nearest agency at which they
might surrender. The closest of any of the Sioux winter
camps to the agencies was over two hundred miles away.
The big main camps of the Hunkpapa and Oglala were
even farther out across the snowy plain. It was a cruel
deception to tell those Indians that they must come in to
the agencies by the last sun of January. For the messengers who were sent out from the agency to bear this
order to the hostile Sioux had not even reached the main
camps when the January moon was finished.

Not one of those messengers is known to have found
any winter camp of the Sioux in time to permit the latter
to travel through the deep snows, even had they wished
to do so.

The Sioux understood this clearly.

They were not ignorant. They knew now that the
white man intended to destroy them. The white man
said, "Go to the agency at once, or the Pony Soldiers will
hunt you down and make the snow bloody where they
find you." At the same time, the white man knew that
the Sioux could not obey his order.

Now, certainly, the Cheyenne must join the Sioux.

But, to the amazement of the latter, the people of Two Moons still said no.

"That paper of the Grandfather's," replied Two Moons, "does not say anything about the Cheyenne. It names only the Sioux. We are still at peace. The Pony Soldiers will not bother our camps. It is the Sioux they want."

The Grandfather, or the Great Father, was what the Indians called the President of the United States.

Surely *his* word on a piece of paper meant what it said.

Of course the order was not from President Grant. But, in their direct, childlike way, the Cheyenne had come right to the truth. The President, the Grandfather, must know of the order, and so it became as his order, even so.

Sitting Bull was at first very angry, then alarmed.

A council of the Sioux was called to meet in the village of the Hunkpapa, high up along Beaver Creek. The chiefs, muffled in their winter robes of buffalo and wolf, came in by ones and twos and threes. All of the famous warriors of the bands still outside the reservations fought the great drifts and the bitter, terrible cold. All were there, save one. Makhpiya Luta—Red Cloud, one-time unquestioned head man of the Oglala—was not among the dark-faced leaders who gathered at the lodge of Tatanka Yotanka. He had gone upon the reservation, and he had taken many of his people with him. The council noted his empty place in the circle about the fire, and the elders nodded to Crazy Horse that he must take that place. He did so, and from that time the Oglala of the wild bands called him their war chief, and Red Cloud was forgotten and his name spoken no more.

All of the chiefs were allowed their turns to speak to the council, and to say what their particular bands would do: whether they would now try to go in to the reservation and surrender, or stay out in the snow and fight.

At last it came down to the time where only Sitting Bull and Crazy Horse had not spoken.

And it came down, also, to this: whatever it might be that these two great men would vote to do, that would be the vote, too, of all the others.

Sitting Bull, when the pipe was pointed in his direction, raised his hand. He did not rise, however.

"My chiefs," he said, "everyone here knows my heart in this matter. Let my Oglala brother speak for me."

All eyes turned upon Crazy Horse.

The legendary Oglala came slowly to his feet. He stood for a long moment without a movement. The firelight fell upon the red-bronze of his fierce face. It glittered within the inky black shadows of his eyes. It bathed in scarlet glow the red Hudson's Bay blanket which swathed his copper body. The silence in that lodge was a thing to be felt by the nerves. It made the skin chill.

Suddenly, from the ranks of the watching chiefs arose a deep sound. *Hun-hun-he! hun-hun-he!* it ran in a growling like thunder around the firelit ring of savage red faces.

Crazy Horse bowed his head.

It was the "courage sound," the guttural rumble that the Sioux men reserved only for the "moment of deepest respect," and it was the greatest tribute that they could pay a man.

"*Ha-ho,* my brothers," the slender war chief said. "I must thank you in my heart, for my words are not enough, nor will they come out of my heart. Let me only say that I will not fail you, nor ever forget that you are my people."

He paused, his slanted eyes, gleaming like hot coals in the shadows of Sitting Bull's lodge, sweeping the circle.

"I will not ask my women and my little children and my old ones who are weak and feeble to march that long harsh way through icy drift and blizzard wind to reach an agency where no food awaits them, and no real friendship, either," he said.

"Even as I speak to you here, the lodges of our people on this river, and throughout the other winter camps, are filled with agency Sioux who have stolen away and come back home simply to get something in their bellies more nourishing than the windy promises of the whites."

For the final time he hesitated, then concluded swiftly.

"I will stay out here and be free! I will fight the Pony Soldiers. I will die a Sioux, and I need no cowardly Cheyenne by my side to do that! That is what Tashunka says."

A vote was held at once.

Only one chief found his heart failing him. He Dog, a boyhood friend of Crazy Horse's, led his eight lodges of Sioux out of Sitting Bull's camp and over the deep-snowed ranges to join the people of Two Moons, and follow the path of peace.

For the others, it was the darker road.

With spring, and the new grass, war would come.

A-ah, katela! So be it!

Death to the Pony Soldiers!

12. THE WONDERFUL TONGUE OF THE WASICUN

In their buffalo-hide lodges the Sioux of the Tongue River free bands knew some brief happiness. The weather was very bad, even for that land of bitter snows, but there was plenty to eat and plenty of wood and dried buffalo chips to keep the tipi fires burning brightly. Visitors coming to the wild camps from the agencies during the February moon reported that the Pony Soldiers had been forced to turn back in an expedition they had planned from Yellow Hair's fort over in the Dakotas. The Pony Soldier chiefs had decided that the snows were too deep for white men to march from the *Mini Sosi*, the Missouri River, to the Sioux camps on the Tongue and the Powder and the Rosebud. Was that not interesting, the visitors asked, when the white man thought nothing of commanding the Indians to march through those same deep snows *from* the Tongue and the Powder and the Rosebud, to the *Mini Sosi?*

Ah, the *Wasicun*, the White Man!

What a wonderful tongue he had; it could wag in two separate directions at the same time.

What a pity, too, that the tongue of the *Shacun*, the Red Man, could speak only in a single line.

But, anyway, there was cause for thanks. The good friends and relatives from the reservations had brought welcome news. There would be no Pony Soldiers that winter. The people could enjoy the warm lodges. They could play with the little children. The women could cut and sew the beautiful moccasins and leather shirts for the spring hunting parties. The men could while away the smoky tipi-hours with their endless tales of great fights and fighters of the past. All would be of gay heart, as in the old days, before there were any soldiers.

Owanyeke waste, said the Sioux. Everything was good to the eye, was pretty to look upon.

But the Sioux were only seeing what they wanted to see; believing what their wild hearts wished to believe.

They were not remembering what had happened to Black Kettle and his people in their happy winter camp along the Washita.

The Pony Soldiers had not forgotten that lesson, however.

When the troops from the Missouri River could not get through the terrible snows from the east, other troops were at once ordered to march from the south.

Of these troops the Sioux of Tongue River knew nothing.

Yet the troops had gathered upon Fort Fetterman, down in Wyoming, by the hundreds and hundreds. So swift and so secret was the planning that, by the first sun in March, the new soldiers were moving up the old Bozeman Trail, toward Montana, and the Sioux still did not know that they even existed!

The destination of those troops was the Wolf Mountains and the headwaters of Tongue River.

Their commander was a man feared and respected by the Indians second only to Yellow Hair Custer.

He was called "Three Stars" and "Red Beard" by the Sioux, General George Crook by the white men.

Crook's choice for the command of the winter march did not pass unnoticed by his fellow officers in the West.

Nor, indeed, far back in Washington.

Of course, those loyal to Custer continued to insist that it was only the deep snows which had kept their "Boy General" from being given the chance to strike at the Sioux.

But there were other whispers flying about the nation's capital, not so favorable to the leader of the

Seventh Cavalry. It was not the snows, alone, said these whispers, which had kept Custer from the command.

There was something else involved; something much more serious than the depth of the snowdrifts between Fort Abraham Lincoln and the winter camps of Sitting Bull's Sioux.

13. THREE STARS AND THE MULE-SOLDIERS

The General had been in the East on leave, far from his post in the Dakotas, since the early fall of 1875.

He and his sprightly wife, Libbie, had been doing the town in New York, with Custer showing little or no disposition to return to the snows and the zero cold of the open plains. He continued to ask the War Department for extensions of his leave until, at last, it was February and Crook had been given the task of subduing the Sioux.

Only then did "Armstrong" seem to realize that he had perhaps been at play too long. He made immediate effort to reach Fort Abraham Lincoln and resume his command. But stronger fates outmarched him. No sooner did he arrive at his post than orders from the War Department came over the telegraph wires: General Custer must return at once to Washington to answer certain inquiries of the Congress.

These "certain inquiries" were what had caused the whispers to spring up and say that more than snow had kept him from his "last best chance to chase the Sioux."

Custer, in his honest soldier's way, had spoken loudly about corruption. In particular, one article said to be his pointed the finger of guilt at Secretary of War William W. Belknap—President Grant's soon-to-be-impeached friend. Graft, the taking of money for political favors, was the dark charge leveled in the article. Custer denied authorship, but Grant was completely angry with "the young popinjay" this time. He would not relent of his

directive calling the General back to the capital, despite
all efforts of Custer's powerful friends to get him "off the
carpet."

However, in his usual reckless way, Custer would not
retreat either. His subsequent testimony before Congress was ruled hearsay in its entirety. He was discred-
ited as a witness and excused from further testimony,
but *not* allowed to return to Fort Abraham Lincoln and
his command of the Seventh Cavalry. President Grant
might be, as his critics said of him, "a cigar-chomping,
whiskey-drinking old hellion," but he was something
else, too: he was one of the greatest professional soldiers
in American history, and he believed that he saw, in
George Armstrong Custer, certain weaknesses which
unfitted the Seventh's leader for command of so serious
an undertaking as the final capture or destruction of the
Sioux.

So it came to be that, while Yellow Hair languished in
Washington knowing that his great opportunity was
passing him by, Three Stars Crook, a man who did not
chase glory nor ghost-write articles accusing the President's cabinet officers of "selling Indian agency and
army post traderships," was marching through the snows
of northern Wyoming.

It was some time in the second week in March that he
struck the headwaters of Tongue River, and started
down that stream.

Between him and the camps of the Sioux lay only the
unbroken snowfields and the dark-timbered sentinels of
the Wolf Mountains. He crossed into Montana, still
undiscovered by the Sioux. His chief scout, Frank
Grouard, told him to keep going, to move even faster.
Crook nodded, and passed the order: forward, *ho*,
double time!

There was good reason for this trust in Grouard.

The dark-skinned scout was a half-breed of strange
beginnings. His father had been a Frenchman, his
mother a native of the South Seas. From her he took the
dark skin and the features which later were to save his

life, for finding him, as a young boy, with a wagon train of white emigrants, the Sioux believed him to be an Indian, and did not kill him. Instead, they took him to the Hunkpapa camp of Sitting Bull, where he was raised in the very tipi of the medicine man and vision-dreamer who now led all of the Sioux in Red Cloud's place. To Sitting Bull, Grouard was as an own-son. He was given the name of Sitting-with-Upraised-Hands, and the nick-name of "The Grabber." When, as he reached manhood, Grouard had returned to the people of his white father, it had been a great blow to Sitting Bull, and indeed to all the Sioux. As yet, however, the Oglala and Hunkpapa did not realize that The Grabber, whom they had raised as their own blood, was actually working for the enemy, against his fierce foster-parents—in the employ, even, of the detested Pony Soldiers!

Hence, when, upon the cold and snowy morning of the 14th of March, 1876, three young Sioux braves halted their snow-caked ponies on a windy ridge above the frozen Tongue, they received a very bad surprise.

It was shock enough to see, down there in the valley, the long dark line of mule-mounted foot soldiers, cavalry-men and army ammunition wagons crawling northward along the river toward their winter camps. But the more ugly discovery was yet to come.

The leader of the three braves was an Oglala. His two companions were Hunkpapas.

Little Killer, the Oglala, owned a pair of army field glasses which he had taken from a dead officer. Through these, he now commenced to examine the rapidly moving column of strange Pony Soldiers who rode mules into his country in the dead of winter.

His first discovery was that Three Stars Crook headed the enemy troops. That was enough bad news to bring frowns and growls of uneasiness from the two Hunk-papa. But then the young Oglala made a hissing sound and uttered the warning word, *a-ah!* and handed the field glasses to one of the Hunkpapa.

"Look down there riding with Three Stars," he said. "See who it is that guides these *Wasicuns* against us."

The Hunkpapa took the glasses, focused them.

"*Howo!*" cried the Hunkpapa. "It is The Grabber——!"

The Indians then knew they were in very great trouble, and must act with all haste. Yet they must take great care, too.

"I will stay and follow the soldiers," said Little Killer. "The one of you must ride to warn the village of Sitting Bull, the other to carry the alarm to the lodges of Crazy Horse. *Hopo, hopo,* hurry now!"

"*Ha-a-u!*" said the Hunkpapa, and turned their ponies from the ridge and were gone down its far side, racing north.

Little Killer waited on the wind-blasted spine of the ridge until the last mule-soldier had vanished beyond the bend of the Tongue. Then he put the heels of his bull-hide moccasins into the shaggy ribs of his spotted pony, and sent him down the slope, into the valley.

"*Hookahey!* small horse," he said with fierce softness. "Let us go swiftly after them!"

14. THE FATAL TRAIL OF HE DOG

Little Killer followed the column of Three Stars Crook only a short way down the Tongue. Then, surprisingly, the mule-soldiers stopped. The Grabber had halted them.

The Oglala brave watched through his field glasses.

Grouard was excited. He kept pointing away from the Tongue, over the high country toward Powder River. That was very interesting, thought Little Killer. Over there on the Powder was the winter camp of Two Moons and those "peace lovers" of his, those Cheyenne who would not fight.

Was it possible that The Grabber was telling Three Stars to go after those Indians?

How was that possible? They were peaceful Indians.

When He Dog and the eight lodges of his Oglala had deserted the camp of Crazy Horse to go with the Cheyenne, it had been because Two Moons had already sent his word to the agent at Standing Rock that his people wanted peace and would come in to the reservation in the spring.

He Dog believed, through this, that if he were found with the Cheyenne, he, too, would be called peaceful, and his people would be safe from the soldiers. In the spring he planned to surrender with Two Moons and the Cheyenne. Now these soldiers from the south, from Wyoming, they must know of Two Moons' offer to come in when the snows melted. They had to know. Two Moons had sent his messengers to Standing Rock a long time ago. Something was very wrong here.

Presently, he saw the mule-soldiers turn away from Tongue River. They went over the high country, toward the east and toward Powder River. The Oglala young man sat upon his pony, frowning.

At first he was glad in his heart that the soldiers had not found the camps of Sitting Bull and Crazy Horse.

Then he thought, no, there is still something wrong here. The Grabber had seen something else that Little Killer did not know about. But Little Killer believed that he knew what it was. It must be the trail that He Dog had made, leaving the camp of Crazy Horse and going over the hills to the camp of Two Moons. The Grabber was a great tracker. He was better, even, than any Indian. But he had certainly been fooled here. He had thought that the trail of He Dog and his few lodges would lead him to the main camp of Crazy Horse or of Sitting Bull. And he had thought this because he could tell the tracks of Sioux horses from those of Cheyenne or Arapaho ponies. He was perhaps one of three men in all the prairies and mountains who could do that. The other two were Big Throat Bridger, a white man now grown old, long gone from Montana, and Bloody Knife, Yellow Hair Custer's favorite Indian scout, a full-blooded Arikara.

Yet, great tracker or not, The Grabber had guessed wrong this time. He would not find the Sioux camps over there.

If he led the soldiers along that line of old pony-marks in the snow, he would come to the Cheyenne camp.

Well, what should Little Killer care about that?

If the Cheyenne were harmed, they had it coming to them. Sitting Bull and Crazy Horse had warned them again and again. But wait! Little Killer had suddenly remembered something that caused his heart to beat wildly. His own sister, Fair Morning, had gone to visit relatives in the band of He Dog only three days gone. She would be in that camp with the Cheyenne. What if the mule-soldiers found her there. *A-ah!* Now Little Killer knew what he must do; he must go faster than the winter wind, over those same hills where The Grabber was guiding Three Stars. He must come to the camp of Two Moons before the soldiers did. He must get his little sister and take her away from there.

"*Ho, shuh*, small horse," he said to his pony. "Do not be frightened, but run as though *Yunke Lo* were at your heels. *Hopo, hookahey!* Let's go again!"

The shaggy mustang knew who Yunke Lo was. He was the Sioux god of Death. The pony did not like the sound of his name, and he leaped forward over the icy crust, ears back, eyes rolling.

"*Iho!*" cried Little Killer. "Run——!"

15. THE LEGEND OF LIEUTENANT MOORE

Late in the day of the 16th of March, Crook halted his troops in a deep and darkened vale of the roughlands.

Frank Grouard had found, just ahead, a place where many other ponies had joined those of He Dog's little band.

"Plenty of these new ones are Cheyenne," said the scout to Crook. "But that don't matter. They run together with the Sioux, specially in the winter."

"Now, Frank," said Crook, "we must be sure. We want the Sioux, none other."

"Nothing's ever a hundred per cent sure with Injuns, General," growled the famed guide. "Excepting that you can't trust none of them."

"How far behind then are we, Frank?"

"Closer than I thought, General. I found some campfires at yonder meeting of the trails. Some burning coals still smoking. I reckon your big village is just past them seven ridges due east there. That will put it in the loop of the river, under Sage Mesa. I know the place."

At this point Crook's two senior cavalry officers rode up—Colonel J. J. Reynolds and Captain Anson Mills. Mills was a good steady man, and careful with Indians, like Crook. Colonel Reynolds was neither steady nor a good hand with Indians. He frowned now, seeming very nervous. Captain Mills spoke with an easy, sure manner, however.

"What is it, Grouard?" he said. "The bunch we're looking for?"

"Yes, sir, I reckon it is. I can't tell you for certain sure, until I see their horse herd. I'll know the ponies of the Oglala of Crazy Horse's bunch, even in the dark."

"The dark?" asked Reynolds quickly. "You're not thinking of going after them yet today!"

"Depends on the General," shrugged the half-breed. "I can take you to that village yet tonight, providing you got the sand to follow along." Grouard did not like Reynolds. He thought the colonel lacked the essential quality of any fighting man—a stout heart. But Reynolds ignored the scout's scowling remark, turning instead to Crook.

The latter was still fingering his famous red whiskers. An Indian fighter who had faced all the major tribes in battle, from the bloodthirsty Apache of the Arizona desert to the Comanche of the Texas plain to the wild-riding Sioux of the northlands, he was thinking of his position there in that dark valley with night coming on so swiftly.

"Hmmm," said Crook to himself.

He looked up at the sky, sniffed the cold wind.

"Well now," he said, "I don't see any sense of sending all these weary infantry troops after such a relatively small band of hostiles as these would appear to be. I believe that I smell snow in that quickening wind, too. With a dark night, a rough and dangerous trail, the weather threatening to get worse—hmmmmm."

He paused, and Colonel Reynolds leaped eagerly into the "opportunity."

"I think you're absolutely correct, General!" he said. "We'll camp here and see what is to be seen in the morning, eh, sir?"

Crook cocked his head, bright small eyes gleaming.

"Why, now, Colonel Reynolds, sir," he said in that famous meek-soft voice of his, "I scarcely think that is what I had in mind, at all. I believe what I was going to suggest was that you take the cavalry troops of Mills, Egan and Moore, and go ahead and find that village for us—tonight. I will camp here with the rest of the troops."

Before Reynolds could catch his breath, Crook's voice changed. His words commenced to sing and hop.

Frank Grouard would go with Reynolds and guide him to the village, he ordered. The scout would make certain it was the camp of Crazy Horse's Oglala before any attack. If it was Crazy Horse, Reynolds was to wipe the village out, showing no mercy. But if it were some other Indians, they were not to be touched on penalty of courts-martial.

Getting Crazy Horse was the great thing.

Break him, and the back of the Sioux rebellion would be broken with him. Sitting Bull was not a war chief. He could not continue his resistance without Crazy Horse.

So spoke General George Crook at sundown of the 16th of March, 1876.

Colonel Reynolds only saluted and said nothing.

An hour after sun's last brief light had gone, with the rest of the mule-soldier camp snug and its fires banked for the night, the attack column moved out. Grouard went ahead of the chosen Pony Soldier troops, showing the way. The snow was coming in wind blasts that stung like shotgun pellets. The cold grew deeper with each numbing hour that the men marched eastward toward the Powder. But The Grabber never faltered, never slowed. All through that night the troops stumbled and cursed their way. But with daylight still not yet showing in the east, the half-breed foster-son of Sitting Bull had found the camp of the Indians for them. And more. He had shadowed up to within calling distance of the drowsing village and seen the horse herd. He had *seen* Oglala horses that he knew. This would be the camp of Crazy Horse. Grouard *knew* those ponies, *dead sure!*

Nor was even that all of the good discoveries.

While lying near the pony herd, the scout had heard an old news-crier walking through the village streets and assuring the camp in his rusty-creaking voice that "all was well." The crier had gone on to announce that the scouts which He Dog had ordered to go out and look for the mule-soldiers which the young Oglala, Little Killer, had reported to be coming from Tongue River, those scouts had returned only now. They brought fine news. They had gone a long way toward the Tongue and seen no mule-soldiers whatever. Neither had they read in the snow any sign of Pony Soldiers, or any other soldiers. Little Killer was a very young man. He could be excused for his mistake.

"*Waste, waste,*" the old man had cried. "Go back to sleep, everybody. All is good in the night. *Waste . . .*"

Grouard knew what had happened.

The lazy scouts had not gone "far" toward the Tongue. They had gone only a little way. Had they gone only a rifleshot farther than they did, they must have discovered The Grabber's own tracks, and then, of course, those of the cavalry troops following so closely behind him.

But now the way was clear.

All Colonel Reynolds had to do was tell Egan and Mills and Moore to "Sic 'em!" and the village of Crazy Horse would be done for.

"It will be a beef shoot, Colonel," the half-breed said.

Reynolds knew what a beef shoot was. It was when beef cattle were issued alive to the Indians on the reservations at Standing Rock or Pine Ridge. The cattle were put in a pen where they could not get away, and the Indians would sit on the fence and shoot the poor brutes down with their rifles.

The Colonel shivered and was very much afraid.

But he could not turn back now.

"Captain Egan," he ordered, "mount the attack."

Egan sent Moore's troops to the north of the camp to block the Cheyenne from getting into the rocky hills. He and Mills went in from the south, his troops first, those of Mills to follow in reserve, in the drive to catch the Cheyenne between the jaws of another *wickmunke,* another Pony Soldier trap.

Egan's men charged bravely enough.

They were actually into the camp before an old woman, out gathering sticks for the morning fire, saw the dreaded figures looming through the ice-fog which blanketed the campsite.

Her hoarse cries brought braves, squaws, old ones, children tumbling from their warm sleeping robes in the manner of sowbugs from beneath overturned buffalo chips.

They all ran from the lodges in terror.

At that precise moment, a wind lifted the fog from the bend of the river. The Indians saw the hills all about them alive with the Pony Soldiers of Three Stars.

Yet He Dog, the Oglala visitor, and Two Moons, the Cheyenne village chief, were fighters. Rallying behind the young Oglala warrior, Little Killer, who had seized his loaded Winchester and ran into the streets naked but for his loincloth, they began to fight. Little Killer had shot six soldiers in the space of ten breaths. Egan's troops hesitated. Other Cheyenne were racing up now. The firing became furious at this spot. Frank Grouard, the hated Grabber, was among the first to go down, shot twice-through. The soldiers had not expected such ferocious and instant resistance by Indians who were sleeping in a peaceful camp. They commenced to waver, and soon came to a stop, half in and half out of the village.

"*Hunhe!*" shouted Little Killer. "They are afraid. Quick! Someone must go and get the women and children into the rocks. We have a chance now. See! Up there on the mesa! The other soldiers have lost their hearts. They are just standing up there, instead of attacking like these soldiers."

It was true. Young Lieutenant Moore was still up on the sagebrush flat of the mesa. He had not gotten into the rocks as ordered. He seemed to be afraid, and the Indians sensed it.

"I will get the people together, ready to rush for the rocks up there," yelled He Dog. "You hold back these soldiers down here!"

The Cheyenne redoubled their firing at Egan's troops, while the Oglala chief dashed to the rear. The soldiers began to retreat, then they stood hard and fast. But the time had been enough. He Dog was back now, and yelling that he had all the people ready to go for the hills and get into the rocks. There was a moment's argument about leaving the pony herd, the dearest possession of any plains Indian band. But Two Moons called out that no pony could travel fast through such deep snow. He said He Dog was right. They must run on foot.

"*Hopo! Hookahey!* Come on, follow me!" shouted He Dog.

The rush by the entire Cheyenne village to reach the momentary safety of the rocky hillside now followed.

Too late, the troops of Anson Mills came up in support of Egan's stalled command. Too late, young Lieutenant Moore tried getting into the rocks ahead of the leaping, bounding warriors of the Cheyenne. In the years to come, stories were to be whispered about the army posts of the West that the youthful Pony Soldier was a coward. That in all of the flight of the Cheyenne up that hillside, he and his soldiers did not fire one shot. But the truth was not in that story. The Cheyenne saw what it was that Lieutenant Moore really did, and they honored him for it forever afterward.

As the Indians came upward, their poor women struggling and falling with the papooses on their backs and in their arms, with other children crying out for lost parents but still pausing to help the old people who could not keep up, Moore shouted to his sergeants to pull the troops away and hold their fire. His men formed a funnel through which the entire village fled to the safety of the higher rocks. Lieutenant Moore not only did not fire a shot to stop those Indians, he actually sheltered them from gunfire from below. And, as the red men went by his position, the warriors all touched their brows toward him and called out "*Naonoatamo! Naonoa-tomo!* We respect you! We honor you!" Moore knew not a word of Cheyenne, but he understood the grateful cries as clearly as if they had been shouted in English. He raised his fringed cavalry gauntlet and saluted the escaping red men, and that is the way they remembered him in their legends.

Lieutenant Moore did not stand aside in fear that terrible morning above Powder River. It was not cowardice that guided his heart. It was the love of one man for his brothers.

16. WHAT THE WHITE MAN PAID FOR POWDER RIVER

As had Custer on the Washita, so now Reynolds on the Powder made a bonfire of all the Cheyenne lodges and blankets and food supplies. The red stain lighted the still leaden skies for miles. While the fires were yet leaping and the Cheyenne watched from the hillside, even again like the southern cousins eight snows before, the soldiers took the pony herd and retreated back toward Three Stars and the main force of mule-mounted infantry.

But Little Killer took some reckless young men of Two Moons' people, and went after the ponies. They sneaked in close and cut the wild Indian horses away from the soldiers, driving many of them back to the smoldering village.

Here the people mounted them and the Indian retreat started across the frozen hills, away from the place of the fight which they afterward called "Bloody Snow Bend."

Again it was Little Killer, the Oglala, who showed them the way. Little Killer and the older chief, He Dog.

"Follow us," they told the grieving Cheyenne. "We will lead you to the safe warm lodges of our people. The Sioux will help their Cheyenne brothers. Come on. Sitting Bull has a fine camp along Beaver Creek, over beneath the Blue Mountains. He will give food and fire to you. *Hopo*——!"

So they set off bravely through the bitter cold. More snow whipped down at them from the higher ranges. The temperatures plummeted below zero. Several of

the old people made their last ride that day, and in that
night which followed four small children also died of the
cold. But Little Killer and He Dog said they must keep
on. It was a far ride to the Blue Mountains. And who
knew if Three Stars would come behind them to avenge
the bad fight his soldiers had made?

But no soldiers came after them, and, with that second
nightfall after the shame of Bloody Bend, the people of
Two Moons topped the last ridge and saw before them
the winking of the guide-fires which the Sioux had
lighted to bring them in out of the bleak and stormy
night.

The Cheyenne survivors of the Black Night march
were given everything by the Sioux of Sitting Bull.

The hearts of the Hunkpapa were made to cry, they
said, at what the soldiers had done to their Cheyenne
cousins.

When his people were all being fed and had been
wrapped in warm blankets and were resting by the
Hunkpapa fires, Two Moons went with He Dog and with
Little Killer to see the chief of the Sioux who had saved
his village.

Sitting Bull said that what the Sioux had done was all
that one red man would do for another, nothing more.
But Two Moons shook his head. He told the Hunkpapa
chief that now his eyes were opened at last. Now he saw
that it was but a foolish dream to pray for peace with the
white man. The white man did not want peace. He sent
his soldiers to kill women and children in the dead of
winter—women and children of a tribe which had
promised to obey the Grandfather's order, and to come
in to the reservations.

Now let the white man know that the Cheyenne were
at peace no more. Let the Sioux brother know, too, that
from this fire, the people of Two Moons would fight by
the side of the Hunkpapa and the Oglala, until the end.

Sitting Bull thanked his Cheyenne brothers.

But he reminded them that there was still great
danger from the soldiers of Three Stars. He, Sitting

Bull, must move his camp as soon as the Cheyenne were warmed and revived. They would all go over and camp with Crazy Horse on Tongue River. As they went, scouts would ride out to all the winter camps of all the Sioux bands, calling their leaders to come to the camp of Tashunka Witko and meet there with Tatanka Yotanka, the vision-dreamer.

Two Moons agreed, saying his people would be ready.

Next day they marched, coming without incident to the Tongue and to the site of that great winter war camp where so much of Indian fate was to be forecast.

Present at the council, which sat three days later, were the Sioux White Crow, Gall, Two-Bull-Bear, White Bull, Grey Eagle, Old Bull, Elk Nation, American Horse, Yellow Bull, Black Moccasin, Paints Brown and Iron-Road-Walking.

For the Cheyenne, there were Bob-Tail-Horse, Hump, Comes-in-Sight, High-Back-Wolf, Yellow Nose and Half-a-Horse.

In the center of the circle, alone by the council fire, sat the vision-dreamer who had called them there.

The chiefs watched him as they waited.

Sitting Bull was a short, powerfully broad man. He had a very large head. His face was without much expression, wide of forehead and wide between the eyes. His eye-color was oddly gray, not black or brown like that of most Indians. Also the eyes were levelly set, not slanted or slitted in the usual Sioux manner. His hair was showing the silvered-snows of his considerable number of winters. Seeing him thus, none but a red man could have guessed at his enormous influence and power among his people.

And now he arose to speak.

What he said was brief, but all the chiefs remembered it.

"My brothers," he told them, "the whites are a great lake around us, and the Indians are an island in the lake's middle. We must stand together or they will wash us all away. These soldiers have come shooting. They want war. All right, we will give it to them."

Then it was the turn of Tashunka Witko, of Crazy Horse.

He, too made a picture never to be forgotten.

And he, too, kept his talk short.

"My chiefs," he said, "our uncle, Tatanka, has put the tongue to the words of angered sadness crying in the hearts of us all. A war will come now, and I will lead you in it."

The council then departed after one final instruction from the quiet-faced Sitting Bull.

It was an instruction which cost many a white man his hair. Shot away many a soldier's life. Lost many an innocent white settler his wagons, his horses, his milch cows, even his wife and his children, in the terrible months to come. It was an instruction which smashed Three Stars Crook and his thousand-man mule-soldier column completely to a halt, disorganized, beaten, afraid to move again. It was an instruction, finally, which was to run red with the blood of the Seventh Cavalry the sunlit buffalo grass of that "other river" which waited for Yellow Hair Custer and his gallant men.

"Swift riders will go at once to every hunting band of Indians yet free upon the prairies," said Sitting Bull. "At the same time, riders will go to every agency of the Sioux, Cheyenne and Arapaho to the sunward of the Big Muddy River. The riders will whip their ponies hard. When the ponies stagger at last into the prairie camps and the agency villages, the riders will leap from their backs and will rip open the entry-flags of each chief's tipi, speaking to him these words of Tatanka Yotanka:

"*It is war. Come to the camp of Sitting Bull which then will be at the big bend of the Rosebud River. Let us all get together and have one more big fight with the soldiers!*"

"Hun-hun-he!" roared the chiefs, deep voices bounding from the buffalo skins of the council lodge. "Let us die as proud men, as free men, as *Indians*——!"

Thus was named the true price of Reynolds' cowardly raid upon Two Moons' sleeping camp.

That price was not the destruction of the Cheyenne lodges and the death from cold of a few old people and little children at Powder River a few days before.

That price was the death of two hundred twenty-six helpless officers and men three months later.

For the name of that waiting "other" river was not the Rosebud or the Powder or the Tongue.

It was the Little Big Horn.

PART FOUR

THE ROSEBUD

17. GENERAL GRANT SURRENDERS

All of this while, Custer had been back in the nation's capital fighting for his political and military life.

Not only had President Grant refused to let him return to his command, he also had issued direct orders to General Alfred Terry that Custer must not be permitted, *under any circumstance*, to even go with the troops of the Seventh Cavalry when that spring's great column of soldiers should march from Fort Abraham Lincoln.

It was no secret now, except to the unsuspecting red man, that a great expedition was to be launched against the hostile Indians as soon as the snow was gone and the prairies were open to travel by land and river.

General Crook had failed badly in his single-handed attempt to crush the Sioux. He had done worse than fail; in the order which sent Reynolds against the village of Two Moons, Crook had been responsible for getting the Cheyenne into the war on the side of the Sioux.

General Terry, an old rival of Crook's, saw in Crook's bad luck a rare chance to build his own reputation as an Indian fighter. There was only one flaw in the opportunity: General Terry was *not* an Indian fighter.

However, Terry knew where such a fighter was to be found.

The place was right in his own command at Fort Abraham Lincoln. The man was one who had chased more Indians—yes, and caught more of them—than any other cavalryman on the plains. And this did not exclude the famous red-bearded Crook, General Nelson A. "Bearcoat" Miles, Captain Anson Mills or any of the army's skilled western officers. The only problem was to convince President Grant that he, Terry, must have this particular "Indian hunter" by his side, if he were to do better against the Sioux than had Three Stars Crook.

Toward this end, two fateful letters were written in early May. By this time, President Grant had relented enough to permit Custer to return to his post. Indeed, the reckless commander of the Seventh Cavalry had proceeded there *without* permission, when Grant refused to see him personally in Washington. But the first week of May had begun with no word that Yellow Hair would be forgiven. And the latter knew that the time was already growing much too late for the troops to be setting forth against the Sioux. The ponies of the Indians would be too strong and fat, the Indians themselves too full-fed from the spring buffalo hunts, to make for an easy victory over them. So the two letters rolled eastward along the rails of the Iron Horse bearing seals and signatures warning of their vital nature.

The President was handed the communications from the West by special courier, and his bulldog jaw clamped down hard upon the ever-present cigar.

This is what he read:

HEADQUARTERS DEPARTMENT OF DAKOTA
SAINT PAUL, MINN., MAY 6TH, 1876
ADJUTANT GENERAL,
DIVISION OF MISSOURI, CHICAGO.
(*I forward the following: To*
his Excellency the President
through military channels):
I have seen your order, transmitted through the General of the Army, directing that I be not permitted to accompany the expedition about to move against the hostile Indians. As my regiment forms a part of the proposed expedition and as I am the senior officer of the regiment on duty in this department, I respectfully but most earnestly request that while not permitted to go in command of the

expedition, I may be allowed to serve with my regiment in the field.

I appeal to you as a soldier to spare me the humiliation of seeing my regiment march to meet the enemy, and I not to share its dangers.

(signed)

G. A. CUSTER

BVT. MAJ. GENL. U.S. ARMY

The second letter was only a brief note in support of the first. But it was eloquent and Grant understood this fact.

Sir:

In forwarding the above, I wish to say expressly that I have no desire whatever to question the orders of the President or of my military superiors. Whether Lieut. Col. Custer shall be permitted to accompany my column or not, I shall go in command of it. I do not know the reasons upon which the orders already given rest; but if those reasons do not forbid it, Lieut. Col. Custer's services would be very valuable with his command.

(signed)

TERRY

COMMAND DEPARTMENT

When he had finished reading, Grant's cigar had gone cold.

His troubles were many in those latter days, and he was weary of them. He knew by this time that Belknap, his Secretary of War, was in a grave situation. He knew, too, that what Custer had said of corruption in the War Department was undoubtedly true. Himself as honest and courageous as any man alive, Ulysses Simpson Grant knew also when to admit a wrong, and when he must redress it.

General Terry wanted Custer.

Grant did not trust Custer, nor did he believe him to be a sufficiently good and careful commander for the moment's grave assignment—he had not changed his mind in that.

But he was too big a man, and too just, to think that he might unfairly damage a fellow soldier's reputation for reasons of personal dislike, or professional pettiness.

"Mr. Secretary," he sighed to the slender man hovering at his elbow, waiting for his reply, "you may telegraph General Terry and tell him Grant surrenders . . ."

"Custer's Luck" again!

In the face of all odds, Yellow Hair had regained command of the Seventh Cavalry. He would go with Terry toward the Rosebud, even as Crazy Horse would go with Sitting Bull.

The trumpets of the Pony Soldiers would blow in the same spring wind with the beating of the Sioux war drums.

Where would the two sounds meet?

And when?

18.   THE GIRL HE LEFT BEHIND HIM

The seventeenth of May, 1876, was a day as fine as
springtime brings to the great plains country. The
weather was clear, warm, heady with the smells of
prairie flowers. The gates of Fort Abraham Lincoln were
lined with cheering wives and children of the proud
troops marching away to punish the hostile Sioux and
Cheyenne. The regimental band of the Seventh Cavalry
was playing "The Girl I Left Behind Me," and the
officers' ladies on the verandas of their barracks homes
waved linen kerchiefs and cried out farewells as confident as those of the enlisted men's womenfolk.

Of course the General's wife, the spoiled Libbie
Custer, had to ride with the column that first day. She
was a person, then and later, who never saw anything in
her "Autie" but a knight-errant of purest snow-white
purpose.

As for Custer, he treated his wife like a small child,
embarrassing his staff constantly. But then he was "the
General." Terry himself had begged the President to let
him go along. This was G. A. Custer's hour of vindica-
tion, of triumph. If he indulged himself a bit during it,
with such complete nonsense as having his doting bride
tag along for a few miles, who might deny him the
privilege?

Certainly not somber Major Marcus Reno, or compe-
tent Captain Frederick Benteen, who rode behind the
Boy General and his "darling girl," sharing looks of
disgust and, indeed, professional uneasiness.

It seemed to them, and to some other grown-up

officers of the Seventh Cavalry, that regimental bands
and perennial child brides had little place in a column
charged by the President of the United States with
settling for all time the Sioux and Cheyenne troubles of
the Far West.

But it was still Custer's hour, and he commanded it.

The camp that night, the first west of Bismarck and
the post, was gay with the sound of music and laughter
and of the troopers complaining with loud good humor
of Custer having gotten them too far away to spend their
money, before paying them. It was true, too. The
General had had the army pay-wagon follow the column
out across the plains, so that the men could not get
drunk when given their pay.

The Boy General was not going to let anything
interfere with his appointment with destiny.

It was whispered by his enemies—of which he had
some even in his own regiment—that "Armstrong's"
ambitions knew absolutely no bounds. He aspired, some
swore darkly, to no less an eventual promotion than the
Presidency.

It was even said that he thought to make of the
present campaign, the stepping stone to that high place.

But if he had those who were not to be captured by his
great charms, he had also the others who swore as
strongly by him as his critics did at him.

Among these were Captain Calhoun, Tom Custer,
Captain Keogh, Captain Weir, Captain Moylan and, of
course, Custer's scouts, the faithful Arikara Bloody Knife
and the white man Lonesome Charley Reynolds.

Next morning, darling Libbie and the pay-wagon
turned back to Fort Abraham Lincoln. Custer and the
Seventh Cavalry marched on, into a sunset from which
they were never to return.

Libbie Custer may have been the last white woman to
see those gallant soldiers.

Certainly, she was the last to wave them farewell.

19. FORWARD, HO! THE SEVENTH CAVALRY

General Terry's column from the Dakotas marched westward day after day. The line of his soldiers, led always by Custer and his Arikara, or "Ree," Indian scouts, and his Crow Indian scouts, stretched for over two miles.

Twelve troops of the Seventh Cavalry rode first. Then came three companies of infantry, a platoon of Gatling guns, and the wagon train. There were one thousand uniformed fighting men in that long and dusty line!

But no time was lost.

Four other journeys had Custer made over these same plains. He knew every prairie-dog hole and buffalo wallow from the Big Muddy to the Yellowstone. He knew the hostile Indians to be near the south shores of the Yellowstone, somewhere between the Little Missouri and the Big Horn. And he knew that, wherever they were, this time they would not escape.

The reason was that two other long columns of blue-clad troops were closing in upon the Yellowstone at the same time as the soldiers of Terry and Yellow Hair.

From the north, from Fort Ellis and Shaw, General John Gibbon, called "Red Nose" by the Sioux, was marching swiftly with four hundred hardened veterans.

From the south, Crook, recovered from his bad scare over jumping the Cheyenne of Two Moons by mistake, was striking once more upward from Wyoming. Three Stars had nearly eleven hundred men, and he was smarting from his blunder on Powder River. He was looking for those Indians with "blood in his eye," and he intended to find them. He had left all of his wagons behind. His foot-soldiers were mounted on tough army mules, moving almost as fast as his cavalrymen up into the Indian country, skirting the Wolf Mountains, driving by forced march for the headwaters of the Rosebud, and the Valley of the Yellowstone into which those waters led.

The troops were now some three hundred miles apart.

But, as they were all marching toward the same point, and toward each other, the distance diminished and the soldier trap closed about the Indians with secret speed.

Or so the commanders believed.

On the 3rd of June, a party of scouts from Gibbon found Custer's forward troops. Gibbon had reached the mouth of the Rosebud eleven days before. There had been no sign of Crook at the rendezvous. The big hostile camps were moving around now. Some were on the Powder, some on the Rosebud, some on the Tongue. Especially on the Rosebud. But there were no Indians whatever along the Yellowstone. General Gibbon would respectfully wait for General Terry. But it was getting very lonesome up there. Would General Terry please hurry?

This news greatly excited Custer.

Suppose Gibbon or Crook should find those Indians before the Seventh Cavalry got on the scene?

They had plenty of men between them to tackle any number of plains Indians. Why, Crook alone, with his cavalry and mule-mounted infantry, could whip all the Indians in Montana and Wyoming put together! This was a very serious thing.

The Seventh must not be late!

But genial, kindly General Alfred Terry was as complacent and unhurried as Custer was anxious and excited.

"Be easy, Armstrong," he advised. "We will get there."

But in his mind General Terry was not so certain, nor

so satisfied. He had seen the sudden nervousness of Custer at the news from Gibbon, and espcially at the word that Crook was "on the loose somewhere and unreported." Had Terry been wrong after all in forcing President Grant to release Custer against his will? Was this likable and charming young cavalry genius a reckless and unreliable commander, as blunt old Grant feared? Terry would have to watch him closely.

Watch him he did, nor was he reassured.

Two weeks of cautious marching followed, during which Custer boldly disobeyed orders to make a scout on his own forty-five miles up the Little Missouri with four companies of the Seventh Cavalry. For such action, salty old General Stanley had arrested him on the Yellowstone expedition of '73. But patient, fatherly Terry told no one of his worries over the "irrepressible Armstrong," except his diary, and that was not read until years later.

But Terry did recall Custer from the front of the column. First news the General had of this was when, upon striking Powder River, the scout duty ahead was given to Major Marcus Reno. Reno's orders read for him to scout up the Powder, cross over to the Tongue, follow that stream back down to the Yellowstone. But steady Reno disobeyed his orders, too! Yet he had reason, where Custer had none. Reno's scout party had struck the broad trail of a big band of hostiles—at least three hundred lodges, said Lonesome Charley Reynolds, who was with Reno—and the trail was so fresh that some of the pony droppings in its dusty track were still warm!

Now all knew that the big camps of the red men were near.

They even knew, now, where the very biggest of those camps must be.

Reno and Reynolds had followed that hot, three hundred lodge trail far enough to see where it led. *Or seemed to lead.*

It was beyond the Powder, beyond the Tongue, leap-frogging the smaller Rosebud.

West it lay.

Due west, and straightaway, *toward the Big Horn!*

Terry now abandoned caution. He ordered the troops forward with all speed to hook up with Gibbon on the Yellowstone at the mouth of the Rosebud. It was June 17th when the Fort Abraham Lincoln column sighted the cross-stream camp of Red Nose Gibbon's Montana men. They were excited also to see, lying in the Yellowstone, off the southern bank—their side of the stream—the famed riverboat, the *Far West.* All flagging spirits of the long march from North Dakota now revived. Sore feet could no longer be felt. Aching seats no longer ached. Hoarse voices rang with cheers up and down the long line of the Seventh Cavalry, and Custer called up the regimental trumpeters to blow "Garry Owen," the battle hymn of the Seventh, as the sun-burned riders charged down into the valley to greet their brothers from far Montana.

But the good feelings took a little chill upon arrival of Gibbon from across the Yellowstone.

Crook was *still* unreported.

And the Yellowstone was still strangely bare of Indians.

Where was old Red Beard, old Three Stars?

And where were Sitting Bull and Crazy Horse and all those hundreds of hostiles supposed to be gathering in this country and swarming the hills of the tributaries of the Yellowstone?

Something was very wrong here.

Custer, of course, would have no part of such stuff and nonsense. What the devil did everyone expect of those Indians, those far-riding red sons of the plains and prairies? That they would have a welcoming committee down there at the mouth of the Rosebud waiting for the soldiers? Standing happily around at the anchorage of the *Far West* singing prayer songs and chanting good medicine poems for the white brother?

How ridiculous!

Those Indians would have to be hunted up. And right away, too. Even now they might be escaping to the west or south. After all, they had shattered Crook once before, and only three months and not very many miles from this same spot, too!

Somebody had to go after those Indians.

"General, sir!" Custer pleaded with gentle Terry. "Let me go ahead! We cannot lie here waiting for Crook to make his position known. We must at least *find* the Indians, sir, before they find us. Once they get the wind of us, General, then we will never see them again. Tonight. We can go in two hours!"

This was on the day of arrival, the 17th.

For three interminable days Terry hesitated. Then, upon the 21st, a signal from the steamer *Far West* announced that "General Custer is wanted aboard."

Custer knew that Gibbon and Terry had been on the steamer arguing strategy the entire day.

What did they now want of him?

He was rowed out into the stream and put over the low rail of the riverboat. A trooper showed him smartly to the Captain's quarters, where Terry and Gibbon were waiting.

Terry spoke in his patient reticent way.

The two commanders had spent the day going over all scout reports current to that hour and poring over the military maps of the Yellowstone, with the result that the whereabouts of the main Indian camps had been narrowed to two locations.

They were either directly above on the Rosebud itself, or they were over along the Big Horn, or its branch, locally called the "Little Horn."

As to the best estimate of strength of the combined Cheyenne and Sioux forces presently in the country, the scouts believed it could not exceed by far one thousand warriors.

At this point Custer's pale blue eyes flashed.

"Begging your pardon, General," he interrupted. "My two best men—the Ree, Bloody Knife, and Charley Reynolds, my chief white scout—have given me a slightly different count. They say no less than fifteen hundred fighting braves!"

Gibbon shrugged.

"In any event, General," he said to Custer, "there are not so many that a regiment of cavalry cannot handle them."

Again the pale eyes gleamed.

"That, sir, is correct!" snapped Custer. "*If* you are speaking of the Seventh Cavalry Regiment!"

Terry smiled and nodded. This fellow Custer had to be admired. Whatever doubts he may have given a man on the outward march from Fort Abraham Lincoln, to see him now, the light of battle in his thin face, the devotion to duty burning in those unforgettable blue eyes, ah! there was a cavalryman to ride with! No wonder the Indians feared him. No wonder the other officers in the army envied him. Here was a man to reckon with, and to remember.

"Well, General," the white-haired officer said softly to Custer. "I am pleased that you feel as you do. For General Gibbon and I have a little detail for the Seventh Cavalry, and I believe that you will find it to your liking, as well as suited to your particular experience."

He paused, enjoying Custer's visible high excitement.

"I am going to have General Gibbon use the *Far West* to ferry his men over to this side of the stream. They will then march up to the Big Horn, turning up that stream, south. The steamer will accompany them as far as it may find navigable water. I myself am too old for this sort of walking and will command from the *Far West*. Is that clear?"

Custer slapped the map-table with his folded gauntlets. His high voice rose higher still.

"Yes, yes, of course it is!" he cried. "But what of the Seventh? What of *me*?"

"Oh," said Terry, enjoying his small joke, "yes, you."

Again he paused, then waved his hand as if ordering a mere changing of the guard, or a barracks inspection.

"You, General," he said, "will take the Seventh Cavalry and go after those Indians whose trail Major Reno found upon the Rosebud. You will have your written orders in the morning. Good night, sir. Have a good sleep."

20. THE RETURN OF
RAIN-IN-THE-FACE

Around the clock the hostile war camp at the Big Bend of the Rosebud seethed with activity.

Arrivals and departures were endless.

Warriors left for the trading posts and the agencies to barter for guns and ammunition. Others went to the peaceful tribes of west and south to trade for fresh war ponies. Riders traveled to all points of the Indian compass carrying the vision-words of Sitting Bull: "*It is war; come to the Rosebud.*"

Old men started from the camp with empty pack trains, returned with ponies staggering under loads of dried buffalo beef, robes and blankets, new moccasins, harness, bullhide for war shields. Squaws trailed away with empty travois behind their pack horses, appeared again with the animals pulling bulging travois of agency-issued goods: flour, salt, sugar, army blankets, cooking pots, steel knives, axes.

And always the new bands of warriors kept coming, and coming, and coming.

The arrival of one such group of men answering the call of the Hunkpapa vision-dreamer was of singular importance. It impressed the people with the power of Sitting Bull's medicine. *Look!* they said. *See what he can do!*

The newcomers were a small band of Oglala, and they were agency Indians. There were no women or children with them. They were all young men, all heavily armed. In their lead rode a young giant of a Sioux, revealing in his carriage the bearing of a hereditary chief, and also something strikingly familiar in the lines of his handsome face.

As he brought his warriors into the great camp, he was recognized by an old Indian, also from the agencies.

"Jack Red Cloud!" cried the old fellow, and rushed to the tipi of Sitting Bull with the news. "Come out, Uncle, come out!" he cried to the medicine man. "See who your magic has brought to fight with us against the white man!"

Sitting Bull, who was within counciling with Crazy Horse, came to the door of his lodge. Behind him, Crazy Horse peered out to see the cause of the commotion. The young Oglala warrior rode up and saluted the two great men with respect.

"*Woyuonihan!*" he said.

They accepted his greeting, and Sitting Bull said quickly, "Where is your father? Has he sent you to us?"

The young brave shook his head.

"The old man has been to Washington and measured the big guns there with his eagle-feather fan," he said. "He warns we can win no victory against the whites. He advises our people to stay on the reservation. To cover their ears and not listen to the calls of my uncle Tatanka Yotanka. But I would not obey him. I am here. I am ready to fight."

So came the son of the great Red Cloud to join with the people his father seemed to have forgotten.

There was one other arrival, too, in that swarming camp, whose cause and case were of peculiar importance to the hold of Sitting Bull upon the gathering army.

This latter man came on the same day as Jack Red Cloud. Almost, in fact, he followed upon the heels of the magnificent young warrior. But this other one was no younger fighting man, no son of a great man. He was a great man himself, and he had an amazing and fateful story to tell.

Many moons ago, in the first of the new year—no, it was the old year, last year—this man had been seized by Custer's troopers when at peace in the agency store at

Standing Rock. The troopers had come in the night, guided by Lonesome Charley Reynolds, commanded by Yellow Hair's brother, Tom Custer. They had taken the man back to Fort Abraham Lincoln and imprisoned him there on the charge of having been the leader of the Sioux who killed Custer's veterinary officer and the sutler Balarian in the Yellowstone defeats of Custer in '73.

All these moons the man had suffered in that soldier jail, and only a few suns ago had he managed at last to escape. What? What was that? Had he actually been the chief who commanded those Sioux who whipped Yellow Hair on the Yellowstone? Had he actually killed Dr. Holzinger and Balarian, as Custer said? Was he guilty?

Guilty! *Ha! Iho!* Of course he was guilty!

But that was not what had made him angry. It was the fact that Yellow Hair had lied about the matter. He hadn't arrested him because of those killings. He had done it because of his shame and anger at being twice beaten on the Yellowstone by the Sioux under this same man. Yellow Hair had a small mind. He was not the great fighter that the Sioux believed him to be. This man, himself, had easily whipped him. Two times over! That was the message he now brought to all his Sioux and Cheyenne brothers—that Sitting Bull was right in his great vision—that the Indians would win a tremendous victory over the Pony Soldiers. This man *knew* that.

He also knew something else.

Something he had learned because he had been in prison right there in Yellow Hair's fort all the time Yellow Hair was getting his troops ready to march west. He knew all about how many troops there were, how good the men were, how many were old soldiers and how many green new boys—he knew everything about Yellow Hair's army. Including the most important thing of all. *He knew where that army was right now,* and he could take a big scout party to it at once, so that the plans of Sitting Bull and Crazy Horse might be made to set a *wickmunke* for those devils of the Seventh Cavalry that they would never forget!

So went the story, and so came to the war camp on the Rosebud the only Indian who had ever beaten Yellow Hair Custer in fair and open fighting: it was Rain-in-the-Face!

His story set the camp afire with new flames of bravery.

Any hesitation which had been slowing the minds or weakening the hearts of the people was now vanished.

The big scout party suggested and led by Rain-in-the-Face was sent out the following day. From the moment of its dispatch and subsequent finding of Terry's and Gibbon's armies approaching their rendezvous at the mouth of the Rosebud, no movement of Custer and his men was without the knowledge of Sitting Bull and the Sioux War Council.

This was something never understood in the white man's stories of the great fight.

And it was something that made the Indian medicine strong as the blood of the bull buffalo.

But it was well that this was so, for within the week of Rain-in-the-Face and Jack Red Cloud's having found the hostile war camp on the Big Bend of the Rosebud, the Sioux had need for strong blood. If they had discovered the approach of Yellow Hair without his knowledge, someone else had discovered the approach to their war camp without *their* knowledge.

It was upon the bright and sunshiny morning of May 16th that the Indians found this out.

That was the morning upon which a small band of scouts—Elk Nation, Little Wolf, White Bull, Yellow Nose—came racing down the Rosebud from upstream —*the opposite direction* from which the Sioux had been watching the approach of Yellow Hair and Red Nose Gibbon.

These scouts were wildly excited.

Three Stars Crook was coming from the south! He was less than one pony ride away! *Hopo, hookahey* ——!

Tashunka Witko, Crazy Horse, the great strange man of the Oglala, at once asked for more information. He knew how his own people were. Always exaggerating. Always making a big story out of a little one. Like small children.

"You," he said to White Bull, "you tell me. You are of the blood of Sitting Bull. You would not lie to me."

White Bull replied that he and his three companions did not lie to anyone. Three Stars was just over the hill, just up the river. Why would he be there but to fight?

"Yes," said Crazy Horse, "but we have easily beaten him one time already. We and the Cheyenne of Two Moons did it on Powder River *without* any warning. Why, then, are you all so excited now? That is my question."

White Bull drew himself up to stand tall and proud.

"You have a good question, my chief," he said. "And I will give you a good answer for it. Yes, the Cheyenne, with old He Dog's help, did rally and beat back the mule-soldiers that other time. But that was different. This time Three Stars comes riding with Indians helping him. In front of the mule-soldiers we saw over two hundred of the cursed Shoshone scouts, led by Washakie. *Now* do you say we are too excited? *Iho!*"

Crazy Horse apologized. This was dark news indeed. It was the first the hostiles knew that the Grandfather in Washington had at last agreed to let the Pony Soldiers employ Indians to fight against Indians. For a long time the people who were the friends of the red man had succeeded in preventing this inhuman use of red brother against red brother. Now the great fighter understood that all of the days that followed would be different than Sitting Bull had said. When Indian fought Indian, the end could not be far off. But he would not say this to White Bull, or to any of the people. He *must* believe in the vision of Tatanka Yotanka, and so must the people.

"All right," he said to the four scouts, and to the warriors who were now rushing up from every part of the camp. "Let everyone get ready. I will lead the fight myself."

But his heart was not good within him when he said it.

Crazy Horse was seeing a vision of his own now.

It was a dark dream, and in it the bodies of the fallen which lay everywhere upon the ground were not the bodies of white soldiers.

They were the bodies of Indians.

And among those bodies Crazy Horse saw one that he knew better than any.

It was his own.

21. THE RETREAT TO GOOSE CREEK

The battle with Crook next morning on the Rosebud was a wild Indian fight from first to last.

It began with the four scouts who had discovered the return of the mule-soldier chief, given the honor of leading the charge. The Sioux and Cheyenne, by acting so swiftly to strike before they might be found, caught Crook entirely by surprise. The red-bearded general and his men were not ready to fight. They were, in fact, spread all over the little meadow in which they had camped for the night. Every soldier's mule and every officer's horse was unbridled and grazing. The men were lying about on the ground resting. Parts of the command were on both sides of the river. The Indians should have had a sweeping and terrible victory.

But they made the mistake of underestimating Crook.

The four scouts, peering over the hill in the forefront of the red attack, were excited.

"Look!" cried Yellow Nose. "Look down by the spring there. Old Three Stars is still braiding his whiskers!"

Sure enough, there was General Crook taking his ease by the side of a lovely little fount of water. He was carefully weaving his famed beard into two queues, tied with ribbons! This was to keep the whiskers from blowing in his face in the attack he was expecting to make on the Indians later in the day. He always did that before a fight, the Sioux understood. He even used the same mirror for good luck. This was a polished frying-pan bottom. It was being held up for him now by an enlisted man, so that he might see if he were ready to mount-up his mule-soldiers and lead them into battle.

"Yes," said Little Wolf. "And see also that he wears his canvas tent as usual, *iho!*"

This was the Sioux or Cheyenne description of the patched army fatigue uniform which this great general wore on his campaigns. Along with his braided red beard, it was his trademark, letting the Indians know that he had surely come to fight, not just ride through their country.

"The men have all eaten their breakfasts," commented Elk Nation pleasantly. "Isn't that a nice thing? You know that a man always dies more happily with a full stomach."

White Bull scowled. They were wasting too much time.

"*Hopo!* come on," he ordered. "Let's get back, or someone will start the charge without us."

But they were already too late.

Washakie's Shoshone scouts, out early in the dawn, had just returned to the halted column. In the process, they saw the four scouts turning their horses from the hilltop.

They charged the four hostiles, chasing them hard.

And when they rode over the top of the hill, there on the far side, they saw the thousand warriors of Crazy Horse waiting to pounce on Three Stars and the mule-soldiers.

The Shoshone hated the Sioux.

Instead of running back to the white soldiers, they instantly attacked the entire Indian army. The hostiles were disorganized by this charge of over two hundred fierce men of their own blood, armed with repeating Winchester rifles.

They became momentarily scattered and the Shoshone scouts were then able to retreat to the column and find that their brief bravery had given Three Stars time to get most of his command into the bluffs and protective rocks of the river.

From there, the hostiles tried in vain to dislodge

them. The fight raged for hours and until late in the day, when, at last, the weary soldiers began to draw back from the rocks. They were breaking and would be running in full retreat in another few minutes. It was then it happened.

Out of the hills on the far side of the river, behind the attacking Indians, a cavalry trumpet sounded high and clear. Amazed, the red horsemen whirled to see, splashing across the shallows of the Rosebud, Captain Anson Mills and eight troops of Pony Soldier cavalry. *Aihai!*

They had not yet realized that Mills and the horse-mounted Pony Soldiers had separated from Crook. Now they discovered their carelessness too late. Mills had been dispatched to find their village while Crook and the mule-soldiers fought by the bright-watered spring. *That* was why they had so easily unbraided Red Beard's whiskers—not because old Three Stars was becoming soft in his brain.

Well, enough blood had flowed anyway. Old Three Stars had been hit very hard. He was in no condition to be helping Yellow Hair Custer and Red Nose Gibbon. The Indians could now turn their eyes on the *real* enemy, on Yellow Hair and the Seventh Cavalry. *Hopo! Hookahey!* Ride back to the village. Get ready for the big scalp dance tonight!

The Sioux and Cheyenne pulled away from their chase after the fleeing mule-soldiers of Crook. They knew Captain Anson Mills for a fierce and hard fighter, and the Pony Soldiers of his looked mean and angry. Away went the red warriors, shouting, yelping, crying their war cries and blowing their eerie chants on the eagle-bone flutes which were the "bugles of the red cavalry."

The battle which was to become known as "Crook's Fight on the Rosebud" was over.

But its effects were only beginning.

When Sitting Bull heard of the outcome of the clash between Crazy Horse and Three Stars Crook, he forbade any great celebration. "This is not the fight of my vision!" he warned. "In that dream I saw hundreds of white

soldiers all dropping suddenly dead in rows around my
feet! Today you killed but a few, although wounding
many. Listen, now, to me. The place for the great fight is
not this river, not the Rosebud. I will lead you now to
that other river!"

The warriors were disappointed, but they obeyed.

The medicine of the Hunkpapa vision-dreamer was
too powerful to stand against. Moreover, Tashunka
Witko, their great war chief, would hear of no argument
against his uncle, Tatanka Yotanka. He believed Sitting
Bull's vision, he said. All who were of the same heart
must come with him, must go and move the camp to that
other river. Right away!

When he spoke, not one warrior, or one squaw, not
even one child or an old person, turned away.

"*Hun-hun-he! Hun-hun-he! Hun-hun-he!*" they cried
as one.

And the great camp in the Big Bend of the Rosebud
River was broken that same evening, and moved off
through the black hours of the night even while Three
Stars Crook was ordering his beaten and frightened
mule-soldiers to retreat all the way south to Goose
Creek, where they sat in fear for seven weeks—licking
their wounds and lying to themselves about what had
happened to them.

The only question that Crazy Horse ever made to
Sitting Bull's order to move the war camp away from the
Rosebud came when the great lines of pack horses and
mounted people were streaming out of the Big Bend,
not yet knowing their destination.

"My Uncle," said the war chief, pulling his pony in
beside that of the medicine man, "where is that other
river that you would have me lead the people to? What is
its name?"

Sitting Bull nodded, and spoke.

"Its name is the Greasy Grass," he answered. "That
stream which the white man calls the Little Big
Horn . . ."

22. FROM THE ROSEBUD TO THE GREASY GRASS

The march of the hostiles toward the Little Big Horn was a thing such as no Indian then alive had seen.

The first dawn was the 19th of June.

The course lay through the most beautiful of all the prairie uplands, the northern foothills of the Wolf Mountains. The summer grass stood high, brushing the moccasins of the riders. Groves of yellow-green cottonwood trees sheltered the splashing waters of the mountain streams. Fragrant pines covered the ridges and mesas. Upon the lower hills were brilliant stands of oak and sycamore, of alder and aspen. Near the water, always, were the slender white trunks of graceful birch. Above all loomed the distant high peaks of the "Shining Mountains," the magnificent snow-clad Big Horns.

Through this paradise moved the Sioux and the Cheyenne with all the lordly pride of hereditary owners.

In the lead, with Crazy Horse, rode Dull Knife and Two Moons, the principal Cheyenne chiefs. Sitting Bull, whose own Hunkpapa people had already removed to the Little Big Horn before the fight on the Rosebud, had held back to accompany the Oglala and the Cheyenne. He rode behind the three fighting chiefs, where all the people might see him and know that he was with them.

Next came the warriors of both tribes mounted on their finest ponies, their buffalo lances splendid with dyed eagle and heron feathers. After them came the vast concourse of pack animals loaded with tipi skins, lodge poles, robes, blankets, pots, pans, spare weapons—all the housekeeping supplies of the wanderers of the high plains. With these animals were all the squaws, old people and young children, together with the scores of yapping curs which always infested every Indian village, moving or still. Lastly, came the immense pony herd of the combined bands. There were three thousand animals—blacks, bays, grays, pintos, chestnuts, roans, whites, buckskins, every color and size and shade known to horsedom. On all sides of the column and in its rear rode the Fox Lodge soldiers of the Oglala Sioux—the Indian policemen who guarded and controlled every large march or movement to the people.

The squealing and kicking of the ponies, the braying of the pack mules, the yelping and fighting of the dogs, the cries of children, yelling of squaws, war-chanting of braves, and shouted orders of the Fox Lodge police—all created a din which might be heard for miles.

The dust raised up into the clear summer skies towered hundreds of feet high. The marching Indians stretched over the low foothills and meadowland valleys for a distance of three miles!

And these were but *two* of the many bands of hostile red horsemen forgathering at the word of Sitting Bull upon the banks of the Greasy Grass.

This fact was impressed upon the Indians themselves when, late the following afternoon, June 20, they straggled over the final rise and saw below them the shining waters of the Little Horn.

There before their startled eyes lay the greatest Indian camp in all *Shacun* history.

To the southeast, upstream toward the Big Horn Mountains and the scarps and gullies of the Rosebuds, were pitched the lodges of the Hunkpapa, together with the Two Kettle, Santee and Blackfoot Sioux bands. After them, going downstream toward the Yellowstone, were the Minniconjou Sioux and the open space reserved beyond them for the Oglala. Next came the tipis of the Sans Arc Sioux and the Cheyenne, the giant encampment stretching both ways beyond the reach of the sight of the staring red chieftains upon the rise.

But merely those Indians and their animals in view below were of numbers beyond counting. Crazy Horse was stunned.

"Uncle," he said to Sitting Bull, "I had not imagined the true power of your medicine. I cannot even *think* about so many warriors to lead into battle. And the horses! They outnumber the buffalo and the birds and the fishes. *Howo!*"

Sitting Bull nodded. "There have never been so many red men of fighting age brought together in one place before," he said. "In the way our people count such things, you and I must know that there are at least two warriors for each lodge."

"*Wan howo!*" muttered Crazy Horse. "Four or five thousand men of battle age!"

"Yes, and among that number two thousand must be called *real fighters*, men who have seen war before this."

The two leaders fell silent, looking down upon the great camp which they had called together.

What their thoughts were in that moment, no white man might say. But what that last great camp meant to the white man was a thing no mind might doubt, red or white.

The grim prophecy made so long ago by Captain Benteen on the night before the Washita attack on Black Kettle was being fulfilled. Counting, in the Sioux manner, five inhabitants of all ages for each lodge along the Little Horn, the numbers in that vast camp were almost precisely what Benteen had said would one day wait for Custer.

There were ten thousand Indians gathered along the sunlit banks of the Greasy Grass.

All Yellow Hair had to do was to find them.

PART FIVE

THE LITTLE BIG HORN

23. "IF THE TRAIL LEADS
TOWARD THE LITTLE BIG HORN . . ."

The Seventh Cavalry marched away up the Rosebud on the 22nd of June, 1876.

Custer had commanded "light marching order."

This meant no tents, no swords, no personal trinkets, not even any blankets or other bedding. The troopers would sleep in the ground, or on their saddle-blankets, or sit up in their overcoats. Custer's sole concern was catching up to the Indians.

Toward this end he ordered the Gatling guns—deadly weapons of rapid fire—left behind.

Each trooper took only his bridle, halter, picket rope and pin, nose-bag for his mount, twelve-pound sack of oats across saddle-cantle, and his knapsack of field rations.

The weapons were 1873 model Springfield trapdoor carbines, caliber .45-70, for the enlisted men, .45 Colt revolvers for the officers. Custer carried a special custom-made rifle in addition, as did some of his staff and the newspaper reporter invited to go along "for the ride" by the high-spirited leader of the Seventh Cavalry.

Owing to a review of the Regiment held for General Terry and General Gibbon, the departure was not taken until noon. The day's march was thus but twelve miles, Custer halting the column at 4 P.M. The camp was in a deep flat surrounded by high bluffs. The cliffs were of yellow clay, the only cover a rough type of bullbrush. Officer and man alike wondered why Custer had ordered such an early halt, and in such desolate surroundings. They soon found out.

For the first time the General now revealed to his staff what the written orders of Terry were.

"Gentlemen," he said, "let me read you the pertinent parts of our instructions:

> "Lieutenant Colonel Custer, 7th Cavalry;
> Colonel:
> The Brigadier-General commanding directs that as soon as your regiment can be made ready to march you will proceed up the Rosebud in pursuit of the Indians whose trail was discovered by Major Reno a few days since. . . . You should proceed up the Rosebud until you ascertain definitely the direction of the trail. . . . If it leads toward the Little Big Horn . . . you should still proceed southward . . . to the headwaters of the Tongue, and then turn toward the Little Big Horn. . . . The Column of Colonel Gibbon is now in motion for the mouth of the Big Horn . . . it is hoped that the Indians . . . may be so nearly enclosed by the two columns that their escape will be impossible. . . .
>
> > Very respectfully,
> > E. W. Smith,
> > Captain, 18th Infantry,
> > Acting Assistant Adjutant-General

"So you see, gentlemen," smiled Custer, folding the orders, "we are supposed to get above the Indians while Gibbon gets below them, and so come together as to crush them between us."

He paused, looking at his officers, the famous peg-toothed grin lighting his thin face.

Major Reno, that sober and unsmiling man, could see nothing of great humor in the moment.

Neither could Captain Benteen.

"You're not thinking to add something of your own to those orders, are you, General?" the latter asked.

"All in good time, Captain," he laughed, "all in good time."

He would say no more, and dismissed the officers.

"I think," said Benteen to Reno, as they walked away, "that he has stopped early today to give us strength for what he intends to do wrong tomorrow."

Major Reno only nodded and said nothing.

He had discovered that big Indian trail. His scouts had followed it a long way and returned to tell him that they promised it would lead to more Indians than any cavalry regiment would want to fight. Even the Seventh Cavalry.

He had spoken these worries to Custer, and been waved aside. Reno was a professional soldier. He said no more about it at the time, nor would he now.

"Well," said Benteen cheefully, "one thing's sure; we won't have to wait until tomorrow for a fight. We are going to be battling these pesky mosquitoes all night long! Did you ever see so many of the brutes, Marcus?"

"I never did," agreed Major Reno, brushing away the singing clouds of insects which swarmed the bottomlands at day's end. "But never mind. Men who march with Custer are not still long enough to worry about mosquito bites."

The next day proved Reno to be correct.

The start was made very early, and Custer's orders to the troops tightened the nerves of every man.

No one was to leave the line of march, not even stray from ranks to pick a flower or toss a pebble in the stream.

There would be no discharge of any firearm whatever.

All commands were to be issued by officers' voices, never by trumpeter or by brass-lunged sergeant's yell.

There was not even to be any loud talk or jollying among the men. On the vastly silent plains the human voice could carry to great distances, and the sound of a white man's tongue was sure giveaway in Sioux country.

The troopers were even forbidden to whistle!

By these signs all in the command understood that the regiment, this day, had passed within the lines of the red enemy. Yellow Hair was away from the control of Terry; he was on his own now, and the men sensed that

Custer believed the quarry would be sighted at any turn of the river.

Just before noon the first "Indian sign" was discovered.

The column came to a halt while the Ree scouts of Bloody Knife examined the marks of the travois poles and unshod pony hoofprints in the soft earth of the riverbank.

"Maybeso two day," said Bloody Knife. "We go quick."

When the regiment started on it was with a tingling of skin and those quick, wordless glances men give one another when hunting dangerous game that is near, but not yet discovered. Without command, the intervals between the troops were closed up. The pace of the horses was quickened, along with the breathing of their riders.

During the afternoon, three deserted campsites were found along the Indian trail. At the last one, come up to just at sunset, Bloody Knife felt of the leaves which were on the willow and alder branches cut by the squaws to make the shade shelters or wickiups of the Sioux.

"Leaf still limp," he said. "Curl up but no dry yet."

"Lieutenant Cooke," said Custer to his adjutant, "pass the order to camp here. We have come far enough."

The weary troopers were soon on the ground, too tired to wander. A few, with their officers, bathed in the nearby Rosebud. Captain Benteen, who was trying to catch a trout for his supper, scolded them good-naturedly.

"What is this man's army coming to?" he asked. "Bathing before dinner on an Indian campaign? La-de-dah!"

So ended June 23rd.

The regiment had marched thirty-three miles on that day.

They were forty-five miles from the Yellowstone, as far again perhaps from the Little Big Horn.

But these distances were not what disturbed Captain

Benteen, nor what brought him to seek out Major Marcus Reno.

"Major," he said, when he had found Reno in the twilight of the June night, "are you thinking what I'm thinking?"

Major Marcus Reno glanced about to make sure they were alone. He was a more cautious man than Benteen. And perhaps a wiser one. Satisfied now, he nodded slowly.

"Do you mean about Custer disobeying General Terry's orders?" he asked.

"Yes," replied Benteen. "We were not to follow this Indian trail if it led toward the Little Big Horn. We were to circle wide and come in above the Indian camp."

Reno puffed at his pipe and nodded again.

"Yet here we are," he said, "following the Indian trail. I'll admit I don't like it."

"Marcus," scowled Benteen, "Custer is not trying to *meet* General Gibbon on the Little Horn. He is trying to *beat* him there!"

Major Reno shook his head, puzzled and perhaps a little fearful, but loyal still to his commander.

"I can't believe that, Captain," he said. "I simply can't believe Armstrong would risk the regiment like that."

Benteen was silent a moment. When he spoke, his voice was hard and his eyes were angry.

"He *would*," he said. "You'd better remember that, Major. It may save your scalp."

24. BLOODY KNIFE'S DARK WARNING

Next morning the march resumed straight along the Indian trail toward the Little Big Horn.

At midday a very large campsite was discovered. Bloody Knife, raking in the coals of one of its cooking fires, picked out a black ember. Squatting, he blew upon the bit of charred wood. It commenced to smoke, and then to glow.

"Injun stay here last night," he said, looking up at Custer. "Heap close now. Watch out. Go slow."

But Custer did not "go slow." He ordered the pace of the march increased. However, at the insistence of Lonesome Charley Reynolds, his chief of all scouts, he did send out the Ree and Crow Indian scouts well in advance. What those scouts returned to report about mid-afternoon was chilling.

They had covered many miles but seen not one Indian.

The grass, though, far around on all sides, had been eaten short. An immense pony herd had been pastured here not twenty-four hours since. "Thousands of ponies," said Curley, the handsome Crow Indian scout. Great care must be taken from this point. Clearly, there were ten-times-ten the number of Indians ahead than anyone had suspected.

Custer was not pleased with Curley's words.

He did not like to be "warned" by anyone. Especially when in front of his officers, as was the case then.

Moreover, Curley was not of his staff, but loaned to him by General Gibbon.

"What does Bloody Knife say?" he demanded of his own scout, and turning his back on the Crow.

Bloody Knife was as ugly a man to look at as Curley was handsome. His attachment to Custer was that of a totally faithful dog; he followed the General like his shadow, by day and by night. But now he had to shake his head.

"Me say same Curley," he replied. "Too many Injun up there." He pointed toward the Little Horn. "Crow Injun hate Sioux. Curley no lie to you. Too many Sioux. *Iho!*"

Bloody Knife's mother had been a Sioux squaw, his father an Arikara brave. Bloody Knife knew the Sioux as he knew his father's people. Custer's frown deepened. His drooping mustache seemed to quiver with indignation. His pale eyes darted uncertainly at his waiting officers.

"We will go forward!" he announced stubbornly.

Lonesome Charley stepped forward, moving in front of Bloody Knife and Curley.

"Begging your pardon, General," he said, "but I don't think we will. Here is something else we found in the trail up ahead. It was stuck on a pole atop yonder rise."

As he spoke, the white scout handed Custer something which looked like the pelt of a dead animal. It was reddish brown in color. The hair was long and unmistakably wavy. Custer scowled angrily.

"By heaven, this is a white man's scalp!"

"It is," said Lonesome Charley. "Maybe we had better slow down a bit, General. We've made twenty-eight miles today. It's certain we will have a big fight tomorrow, or next day at latest."

"Very well' answered Custer, in his quick way. "Pass the order, Lieutenant Cooke. Tell the men to make small fires and cook their rations before dark. All fires will be put out and the ashes spread while it is yet daylight."

The grateful troopers dismounted. Long before darkness fell they had put out their fires and scattered the ashes and embers so that no rising sparks or tell-tale columns of white woodsmoke would mark their halting place.

Before retiring, some of the officers gathered with Captain Benteen to share a canteen of whiskey one of the group had brought along from the Yellowstone. It was then about 8 P.M. The canteen was still half-full when Custer's trumpeter, a popular immigrant youth named Johnny Martin, stepped out of the surrounding blackness to inform the officers that General Custer wished the regiment to be formed up immediately: a night march had been ordered.

Benteen and the others groaned helplessly.

Custer had evidently thought better of his earlier decision to be cautious and listen to Lonesome Charley. The General was a man who must have his way, come what would. And his way that fateful night was to drive the Seventh Cavalry in a single-file blind march straight on toward the Little Big Horn.

The start was made just after 10 P.M.

For six hours and until 2 o'clock the following morning, the regiment stumbled and felt its way through the pitch darkness. Then Custer called the halt. The men tumbled from their mounts. They lay down in their overcoats where they were, and slept on the bare rocky ground. Before them, only a short distance, was the long ridge which was the divide between the Rosebud and the Big Horn. With first daylight Custer and his favorite white scout were on top of that ridge. Before the exhausted troopers were fully awake, the General was back in camp and calling his officers to him. It was still so early that the sun was not even into the hill-locked basin where he had halted the Seventh. Its first rays were just tipping the high ridge, and spilling over into the valley of the Big Horn, beyond.

When Reno, Benteen, Keogh, Moylan and the others had answered Adjutant Cooke's summons, and were gathered in the misty dawn about Custer, the latter spoke quickly.

When excited, he had a stammering way of speech, and he was stammering now.

Bloody Knife and Curley, with the very best of their Ree and Crow scouts, had been up on the ridge all night. He, Custer, with Lonesome Charley Reynolds, had joined them there just before sunup. The Indians all said that in the gray predawn they could see the hostile camp along the distant banks of the Little Big Horn. They said it was twelve or fifteen miles away, and the biggest camp any of them had ever seen or heard of in the stories of their people.

Here Custer paused to interrupt himself.

"But you know how Indians are," he smiled. "I stared through my field glasses for half an hour up there, and could not see one sign of any Indian camp. Indeed, I could not even see the Little Big Horn!"

At this, Bloody Knife, squatting on the ground nearby, raised his dark hand. He said something in the deep-growled tongue of the Sioux, and Custer turned swiftly to Lonesome Charley Reynolds.

"What did he say?" he demanded of the white scout.

"He said you would find enough Indians over there on the Little Horn to keep you fighting for two, maybe three, days."

Custer laughed. He was at once his old confident, optimistic self. He put his hand on Bloody Knife's shoulder.

"Never you fear, old friend!" he said. "We will get through them nicely in one day——!"

25. THE PATHS OF GLORY

The Seventh Cavalry climbed the divide and passed over it at about 8 A.M. Before them lay the valley of the Little Big Horn River. Custer was excited.

Captain Benteen and Major Reno, with the other officers, had not seen this view from the divide before.

As they now saw it spreading below them, some of them did not like the situation, at all. The reason for this was that the country ahead was a series of rough ridges and gullies. It looked like a rumpled bedsheet covered with scraggly brush and tall grass. High bluffs of red and yellow clay loomed everywhere. These were washed by the rolling, rough waves of the brush and grasslands. Nowhere could the officers see the channel of the river itself.

Was this what Custer had seen from the crest at daybreak?

Was this *all* he had seen?

Were the trusted Indian scouts of the Seventh Cavalry leading the Pony Soldiers into a trap?

Or had their wonderful eyesight *really* been able to see the stream and the campsites of their wild cousins, where the inferior vision of the white man could not?

Major Reno turned to Bloody Knife, who was riding nearby.

"My friend," he said to the Ree scout, "you must not lie to me. Did you see the camp of the hostile Indians?"

"*He-hau!*" growled the red man. "Yes, me see."

"Then," said Reno, "will you please point the place out to me?"

The white officer thought that he had caught the scout in a trick, for Bloody Knife scowled darkly. But the Ree was only showing his pride.

"Why you think me lie?" he demanded. "Me serve you Pony Soldier long time now. Tongue of Bloody Knife not follow two trails, like tongue of snake, or tongue of white man."

"I apologize," said Reno soberly. He was a good man. He lacked Custer's high spirit and dashing charm. He did not have Benteen's wit and good humor. But Major Marcus Reno was an honest and capable cavalryman. His greatest "fault," unlike the handsome leader of his regiment, was that Major Reno never said more than he meant, or promised the impossible.

Now Bloody Knife stopped scowling, waved his dark hand.

"Me understand," he grunted in his deep voice. "You good Oak Leaf Chief. You careful. You afraid. You smart!"

Even Major Reno had to smile.

Was the Indian telling him that he was wise to be afraid?

That it might be good policy to be a coward that coming day?

Reno lost his brief smile.

"Do you see the camp of your wild cousins now?" he asked Bloody Knife. "Can you show it to me from here?"

Bloody Knife pointed to the west, and a little to the north. Following the direction of his finger, Reno could at first see nothing. But then the Ree uttered one grunting word, "smoke," and the officer at once made out the hazy thin blue curls of hundreds upon hundreds of tipi-fires rising in a line which entended for miles. He turned back to the Ree scout, his sober face pale.

"Was General Custer able to see that smoke?" he asked.

Bloody Knife shrugged.

"Me show him," he said. "Him may see, maybe not see."

Major Reno thought Custer must be told of those smokes immediately. He could not gamble with Bloody Knife's word for the matter.

But when he had ridden forward along the line and found the General, he could not get him to stop long enough to look at the distant smoke.

"Major Reno!" laughed the commander of the Seventh Cavalry, "I was looking at those campfire smokes before you were awake this morning!"

"Yes," said Reno, not smiling back at Custer. "But did you *see* them?"

Custer scowled for a moment. He did not like to be thus questioned by his officers. He always invited them to state their opinions freely, but he nnver took their advice, nor really welcomed it. Yellow Hair followed his own orders.

"Go back to your troops, sir," he now said, "and leave the worrying to me."

But Major Reno did not move.

"General," he said flatly, "do you intend to attack those Indians today?"

"What do you mean by that?" challenged Custer.

"I mean," answered Major Reno, "that General Terry told you to wait for General Gibbon to get into position below this camp. General Terry said we were not to attack until the twenty-sixth, when Gibbon should be ready."

"Well, sir?" cried Custer. "Come, come, say what you mean, man! I've no time for guessing games."

"What I mean, General," replied Reno bravely, "is that this is only the twenty-fifth. You're a day early for your *appointment* with General Gibbon, sir. You should wait for him."

"Hah!" grinned Custer, trying to pass off the unpleasantness of the moment. "Can we help it if old Red Nose is so slow of foot? The Seventh Cavalry was given a job to do, Major. I suggest you get back to your men and help me to get on with that job. Lieutenant Cooke——!"

He turned his horse away from Major Reno, calling

again for his adjutant, Lieutenant Cooke. The young officer dashed up, wheeling his horse and saluting smartly.

"Order the column forward at once," said Custer. "We shall follow the course of that small drybed stream ahead." He pointed to a gully which began nearby, and ran all the way down the divide into the valley below. "Tell the officers to order extreme quiet in ranks. Have Captain Benteen take the advance. He's been spoiling for action."

"Yes sir!" said young Cooke, saluting again. "Beg pardon, General, sir," he added. "What's the name of this stream we're to follow down to the Little Big Horn?"

Custer looked a moment at the frowning Major Marcus Reno.

Then his famous peg-toothed grin spread over his sun-tanned face. The pale eyes danced. Custer was a man incapable of holding resentment. His heart was as gay and brave as his never-failing ambitions.

"Well, sir," he answered the youthful lieutenant, "Lonesome Charley Reynolds tells me that the Sioux call it Sundance Creek. But I think we will change that in honor of the day. For the purposes of the Seventh Cavalry, let's call it Reno Creek. The major needs a little encouragement, eh, Marc?"

Reno sighed and nodded his head in agreement.

He could not resist George Armstrong Custer. And few men could. Now he managed a wan smile, and a small wave.

"General," he said, "you know that if you order me to ride off the top of this mountain, that I will do it."

"Nonsense!" laughed Custer, spiritedly. "Nothing that drastic, Marc. All you need to do is lead your men down Reno Creek to glory and to a colonel's eagle! Think of that, sir!"

What he meant was that, if the battle went well and many Indians were killed, Major Reno would be promoted to Colonel Reno as a reward for his loyal services and blind obedience.

But Major Reno could not think of it that way.

He saluted Custer now, and rode back to his men, as any good soldier must.

Yet he was not thinking of Custer's promise to promote him to colonel. He was thinking of that other part of Yellow Hair's statement. The part about following the banks of Reno Creek to *glory*. And that is what made faithful, steady Major Reno seem to be afraid.

The night before, during the rest halt between 2 A.M. and sunrise, when the Indian scouts had gone to the high divide, Custer and Lonesome Charley Reynolds joining them later, Captain Benteen had come over in the thinning darkness to visit Reno.

Benteen had still been with Reno when the Crow scout Curley, a particular friend of Benteen's, had drifted in through the growing grayness of the pre-dawn. Reno had been startled by the handsome Indian's appearance. But he was far more startled by what Curley had to tell his good friend, Captain Frederick Benteen. It was concerning what Yellow Hair had just told all of the Indian scouts up on the divide.

Curley could scarcely believe his ears. He had been so astonished that at first he could not think what to do. But Curley had been to the schoolhouse on the reservation. He was more *civilized* than the other scouts. He knew more about the way the white man thought.

So it had been that when he heard what Yellow Hair promised the Indian scouts, he believed that the officers in the camp below should know of the promise.

For that reason, Curley had slipped away from the divide and come back ahead of the others. This was his story:

When the daylight began to come and Bloody Knife and the Ree and Crow scouts had said they were able to see the great hostile camp of "the three thousand smokes," Custer had refused to believe them. When the Indians then warned that he would find more hostile warriors than any regiment of Pony Soldiers could fight,

Yellow Hair had still refused to be halted, or even made to go slow.

"Nonsense!" he had cried, in his high-voiced way. "You are seeing things! Your eyes are strong but your hearts are weak! Come along, now. Did you ever lose a fight following me? Oh no, you say? Well, then, let's go!"

But the scouts had just stood there.

Then Yellow Hair could see that he must tell them something more than just to follow him. And he had done so. He told the Indians, both Rees and Crows, that he was putting everything important to him into this one fight with Sitting Bull and Crazy Horse. He said that if he won the fight, if he defeated the Sioux champion, Tatanka Yotanka, the famous medicine man of the Hunkpapa tribe, then a great thing would happen.

It was that Yellow Hair would be made the Grandfather—the President of the United States!

If his brave friends, the Ree and Crow, would go with him and run off the pony herds of the Sioux and Cheyenne, Yellow Hair would not forget their people when he sat in the Great White Lodge in Washington.

This story, which was never to be proved, had stunned Major Reno at the time. But with his customary loyalty to Custer, he had put its report aside as "Indian imagination and lies."

Yet now, riding back along the advancing column of the Seventh Cavalry, he was not so sure.

In truth, he was not sure, at all.

Had Curley lied to Captain Benteen? Was the handsome young Crow only showing Indian imagination? Trying to impress his friend, Captain Benteen, with his faithfulness?

Or was it true that Custer had promised great rewards to his Indian scouts because he could see he had made them nervous and afraid by his own rash desires to win a great victory for the Seventh Cavalry? To make a glory-ride which would make Yellow Hair Custer the next Grandfather in Washington?

Steadfast Major Marcus A. Reno did not know.

But in that quiet June morning before the Battle of the Little Big Horn, he was thinking of a line from the famed poem, Gray's *Elegy;* and it was not a happy line.

What was it Custer had just said—to follow him down the pathway of Reno Creek to glory?

And what was it Gray had said so long ago:

The paths of glory lead but to the grave . . .

26. FOLLOW THE FLAG WITH THE BIG RED "7"

Custer halted the advance only part way down Reno Creek toward the valley of the Little Big Horn.

Officers looking at their watches noted the time to be 10:30 A.M. No sooner had they made this observation than they were startled to hear the bugler blowing Officer's Call. It was the first time in two days that the General had permitted a trumpet to sound. Something big must be afoot.

When they had ridden to where Custer awaited them, they found the commander of the Seventh in excellent spirits.

"Gentlemen," he announced, "we have been discovered by the hostiles. Our Indian scouts have seen their warriors riding along the bluffs above for the past half hour. Undoubtedly these braves were drawn by the dust our horses have been raising in descending the dry water-course. By this time they will have returned to arouse the camp. Since there is no more need for silence on our part, we will proceed in battle readiness. Any questions?"

It was much too late for questions. All of the officers knew that, and none of them answered Custer.

"No questions, sir," said Adjutant Cooke, saluting.

"Very well, Lieutenant." Custer's words were sharp with the ring of command. "Have Trumpeter Martin sound the advance."

Shortly, the Seventh Cavalry was moving forward again.

But mile after mile passed and no sight yet of the Little Big Horn River, or of the vast Indian encampment said to cover its banks. Eleven o'clock passed. Noon drew near, and Custer became nervous. He feared that the Indians were fleeing.

"Captain Benteen," he ordered, "take three troops and the ammunition mules and proceed to the left. Watch for the Indian village. If you see it, pitch into it."

Benteen gave over the advance to Custer, took his three troops, about a hundred and twelve men, and the pack mules carrying all of the spare ammunition for the entire regiment. As he went into the rough country, he turned to Captain Gibson and said that he did not think it wise to leave Custer. He added that it seemed very foolish to have the ammunition all with one group. Captain Gibson said that he agreed, but that Custer was commanding the regiment.

"Let's hope," replied Benteen grimly, "that he is still commanding it tomorrow at this time."

But the rough-humored captain would have felt even more grim uncertainty about Custer's leadership had he been able to hear the next order that Yellow Hair issued.

No sooner were the troops of Benteen's column out of sight in the rough hills to the left, than Custer instructed Major Reno to take a like number of men—three troops —and advance to the right, on the south side of the dry streambed.

"I will stay on this side, Marc," he said. "In that way we shall have three columns spreading out, and the Indians cannot get away from us."

Reno saluted and rode away with his three troops.

Like Captain Benteen, his thoughts were not pleasant ones. But he kept them to himself. It was his duty to do so. If he should show uncertainty, then his men would see this in him, and they would become uneasy and afraid.

Moreover, Custer's five troops of the Seventh Cavalry were in plain view on the far side of the dusty streambed. There seemed no hesitation in the General.

In truth, none of the men in the ranks seemed to fear any danger, or to suspect a defeat. Of course, none of them knew what Major Reno knew. It had not been told among the troops that the regiment's Indian scouts had reported *"three thousand tipi-smokes,"* or *"enough Indians to fight for two or three days,"* or had advised Yellow Hair to *"go slow and be careful."*

All the men in the ranks knew was that the big camp of the hostile Sioux and Cheyenne lay somewhere just ahead.

That being so, they also knew that when their general had found the camp, it would be the last bugle call for old Sitting Bull and that wild-riding fool of a Crazy Horse.

When Custer went after an Indian camp, it was the end of that camp.

So, with the officers worried, the commander absolutely determined to push ahead with all speed, and the troopers convinced that no amount of Indians could stop the Seventh Cavalry, the regiment swung to saddle for the last time.

The clear brass notes of Bugler Martin's trumpet shrilled through the early afternoon.

The "Forward, hos!" of the officers sounded down the long lines of blue-clad, dusty troopers.

The men cheered. Even the horses were excited. They snorted and plunged and kicked up their iron-shod hoofs. In the lead, General Custer's long-limbed thoroughbred "Vic" pranced and whirled and pulled at the reins. Vic was a beautiful stocking-footed sorrel horse, fit mount to carry Yellow Hair, the "Boy General," into battle.

Custer wore his famed black felt hat, with rakish wide brim curled up on one side.

He had donned his fringed jacket of Indian buckskin and the bright scarlet neckerchief which was his fighting "good medicine charm." High boots reached above his knees. His gauntlets were of yellow leather, fringed nearly to the elbow. He rode, as always, with the grace

of the born horseman. Here was a cavalry commander to
follow! A commander who, in all the fierce and bloody
campaigns of the Civil War, had never lost a battle flag
or a single gun to the enemy. A commander who had
more courage than a lion, more luck than a Mississippi
River gambler. Here was a leader who always won!

Forward, ho! Forward, ho! Follow the dust of the
Seventh Cavalry. Follow that maroon-and-white regimental pennant, proud with the big red "7" upon its
centerpiece! Never fear, never falter. Follow George
Armstrong Custer to glory and to gallant victory. Forward, ho! Forward, ho!

The horses moved now at a spanking trot.

Their bright blue saddle blankets with the orange
borders flashed in the summer sunlight.

The riders leaned eagerly in the McClellan army
saddles.

Their rough service boots were tight in the oxbow
stirrups, their hands were sweaty upon the bridle-reins.

The gray horse troop, the black horse troop, the bay
horse troop, the sorrel and the white—all moved more
swiftly to follow Custer toward the last bend of Reno
Creek. Around that bend the valley of the Little Big
Horn would open wide. The Indian scouts had just
returned to tell the General this. All straightened in
their saddles, took a firmer grip on Springfield rifle or
big Colt .45 revolver, as this news swept down the long
lines of the Pony Soldiers.

The Indian camp lay only around the bend!

Then, suddenly, the bluffs of Reno's Creek spread
apart.

The first troops rode into the meadowlands of the
Little Big Horn, following Custer. As if by command
—where there was no command—all the crowding
soldiers of the Seventh Cavalry brought their lathered
mounts to a halt.

Before them were perhaps fifty hostile horsemen
riding wildly back and forth not two hundred yards away!

But that was not what halted the troopers. It was what

towered beyond those first brave Indians, and beyond
the great curve of the Little Big Horn. It was a column
of dust which rolled upward as if from some great
volcano, staining the June skies red and yellow with its
angry swirlings. It continued to grow larger as the
troopers sat and stared at it.

Each man had the same uneasy question in his mind.

If the fifty Indian horsemen they had just discovered
in front of them could raise the dust they were raising
putting on their little show for Custer and the Seventh
how many *other* Indian horsemen must be raising that
great dust cloud beyond the river's bend?

"Holy smoke!" cried one excited trooper to his nearby
comrade. "There must be ten thousand of them up
there!"

His companion nodded. He was feeling his first fear

"We'd best start praying, Ben," he said. "And might
hard . . ."

27. THREE COLUMNS JUST LIKE THE WASHITA

When Custer saw the fifty Indian horsemen dashing away toward the banks of the Little Big Horn, he ordered his Indian scouts to pursue them and cut them down.

But the Ree and Crow scouts, although they far outnumbered the fifty hostiles, would not go.

"Him little bunch Injun only decoy," Bloody Knife told Custer. "Them Cheyenne. You follow Cheyenne, you find Sioux waiting. Heap many. Curley, him say all Hunkpapa this end village. Stay back, be careful!"

But Custer was furious. He ordered the scouts to have both their ponies and their rifles taken away from them. Doing this, he intended to punish them. What he did, instead, was to save their lives.

It was here that the Crow scout, Curley, announced that he would go no farther with a man "whose head is spinning."

He meant that he thought General Custer was behaving as a crazy person, that he had lost his senses.

Lonesome Charley did not tell the General what the Crow scout had said. He did not even dare tell Custer that Curley was quitting the Seventh Cavalry.

For his part, Custer dismissed the matter of the rebellious Ree and Crow scouts. "Let them go," he ordered Lieutenant Cooke. "We must continue forward."

"But General, sir," objected Cooke, "what of the

hostile ponies? Our Indian scouts were supposed to run them off."

"Let the ponies go, too," commanded Custer. "We are wasting time here. Those Indians will get away from us. Here, quick, I want you to ride over to Reno with these orders."

Cooke at once spurred his horse across the dry streambed.

"Major Reno, sir!" he called, dashing up to that officer, "the General sends his compliments. He wants you to ford the Little Big Horn. Once across, he directs that you shall take as fast a gait as you deem prudent and charge afterward, and you will be supported by the entire outfit——!"

Cooke turned his horse, galloped back up the streambed of Reno Creek toward Custer's waiting troops. Meeting Captain Keogh on the way, he stopped and the two officers watched Reno's troops go forward and disappear around the bend of the Little Big Horn. They started on, but before they reached Custer, a lone horseman thundered up shouting for them to wait. It was a scout from Reno. The major had already found the Indians! Just beyond the bend. They were everywhere among the trees of the riverbottom. Beyond the trees, the major could see the tips of the buffalo hide tipis by the hundreds. This was without question the great camp they had been looking for. Were General Custer's orders still the same?

Cooke told the scout that he should tell Major Reno that Custer had already given him his orders. He was to attack!

Meanwhile, Cooke would race to Custer and tell him what Major Reno had found beyond the bend. If there were any new orders, any change of the battle plan, a messenger would be sent at once to Major Reno's column.

And there began the mystery of the Little Big Horn.

Cooke did ride hard for Custer, and Captain Keogh with him. But no man knows if they ever relayed to

Custer the information from Major Reno. And no man knows why Custer then did what he did. For, instead of following up with his main force of five troops to support the three troops of Major Reno, General Custer ordered his command to cut *away* from the Little Big Horn. He led his troopers *out from behind* the troopers of Major Reno, and left Reno's men to their fate. The only possible guess which could be made, was that Yellow Hair had decided to make a big circle and strike the hostiles on the flank, while Reno fought them from in front. It was his favorite Civil War cavalry tactic. It had brought him many victories in that war. Also, it had worked upon the red man. Did Custer think of the Washita in those moments before leaving Reno unsupported to lead his own men into the buffalo grass beyond the river, and into history? Did he remember that he had split the Seventh Cavalry into three columns then? Had struck the Cheyenne of old Black Kettle from three sides at once? Had killed them after that like shooting tame cattle in a pen? Had won the greatest Indian Fight victory up to that time?

Ah! no man would ever know.

That is, no man left behind with the commands of Reno or Benteen would ever know.

For when General Custer took his five troops of the Seventh Cavalry into the rolling hills beyond the Little Big Horn that silent, sunlit afternoon, he galloped into eternity.

Neither Reno nor Benteen, nor any trooper with them, ever saw him alive again.

28. CHIEF GALL CLOSES THE HUNKPAPA TRAP

Major Reno waited uncertainly for Custer's reply about advancing past the bend. But no answer came from Custer.

What had happened to Lieutenant Cooke?

Had he not delivered Reno's message? Had the Indians gotten him? Had he given Custer the message, and Custer chosen to ignore it? And aside from Lieutenant Cooke, what had happened to Custer? His troops should be advancing behind those of Major Reno. Reno should be able to see them by now. But he saw nothing behind him.

Ahead of him, it was another matter.

Reno and his anxious officers looked hard at the vast cloud of dusty brown-yellow haze striking skyward beyond the bend. The small band of Indian horsemen which had met the main column of the Seventh Cavalry had disappeared around that bend by now. They were hidden, with their fellow warriors of the main camp, beneath that dust cloud, no doubt.

"Sir," said Captain French, "we had best do something."

"What we had best do," added Captain Moylan, "is to hit the Indians while we still know where they are—in front of us."

"I agree, I agree," echoed young Lieutenant McIntosh.

Major Reno looked at his three officers. He looked at his two scouts, Bloody Knife and Lonesome Charley

Reynolds, loaned to him by the generous Custer only minutes before.

"The captains are right," said Lonesome Charley. "We can't stay here. The Indians will get behind us."

"Too many Injun," rumbled Bloody Knife in his deep voice, and said no more.

Major Reno sighed as though a heavy weight were upon him.

"All right," he said wearily. "Let us go forward."

The three troops of Seventh Cavalry moved ahead at the trot. As they neared the edge of the rising cloud of dust, they began to hear the chirruping, wild war cries of the Sioux and the Cheyenne. The Indian voices were so many and so confusing coming through the thick yellowish dust that the soldiers did not know which way to look for the enemy. The noises of the warriors seemed to be all around them, like a swarm of angry red bees.

"Reynolds," said Reno, grim-lipped, to Lonesome Charley, "we have struck a hornet's nest."

"They are buzzing right bad," agreed the white scout.

The next moment a breeze stirred down the valley of the Little Big Horn, lifting the skirts of the dust cloud.

Before them, Reno and Reynolds saw more Sioux and Cheyenne than they had thought to be in the entire four-mile camp of the hostiles.

All of the yelling, swift-riding braves were mounted on fine ponies. All were painted for war. All had good rifles. Many of them had new Winchester repeating rifles. These were far better weapons than the old Springfield carbines carried by Custer's men. It was immediately evident to anyone who knew Indians that Yellow Hair had *not* surprised the hostile camp that sunny June day along the Greasy Grass.

Lonesome Charley and Bloody Knife understood this fact at first glance.

It took a high plains horseback Indian hours to prepare for battle. To put on his warpaint. To select and bridle the pony he would ride in that day's combat. To oil his gun, and to load it, and to fill his warbag with extra ammunition. To smoke his good medicine pipe and arrange his good luck battle-charms. To say his Indian prayers to the red gods of his people. To Wakan Tanka for the Sioux. To Maheo, the Allfather, for the Cheyenne. And then, finally, to offer war chants to the heavens, so that the bullets of the Pony Soldiers would fly wide of their marks, while those of the Indians would be guided directly to their targets.

The two scouts with Major Reno's troops, thinking of these things which both knew to be true things, exchanged dark and foreboding looks.

"Major," said Lonesome Charley to Reno, "we had better get out of here, *right away!*"

But he had no sooner issued the hurried warning than his companion, Bloody Knife, flung up his arm, pointing ahead.

"Too late," rumbled the Ree scout in his deep voice. "Injuns all around. No go back. Fight here, or all die."

The white officers could see that the hostile horsemen were not waiting for the Pony Soldiers. They were starting out around both sides of Reno's little band of troopers. In another few moments they would be, as Bloody Knife had just said, "all around." Then it would be impossible for Custer to come to their aid. Something must be done.

"You have got to charge them, Major," said Lonesome Charley. "That will pull them back together and give us a chance to fall back toward the General."

Reno nodded quickly. He was not a brilliant nor a dashing officer. Neither was he ambitious. He did not like to see his men die. Nor did he like to think about dying himself.

But he was no coward.

"*Forward, ho!*" he shouted to the troops, and himself led the advance toward the screaming red men.

For several minutes the Indians retreated. Reno and his three troops moved forward until they were in the clear of the bottomland meadow of the Little Big Horn. Now, for the first time, they could see the countless lodges of the camp running beyond eye's reach, north-ward, downstream, where General Gibbon was sup-posed to be coming with his infantry.

Oh, if Custer had only waited one more day!

How simple it would have been to catch and crush those Indians between the Seventh Cavalry and Gib-bon's foot-soldiers and his artillery cannon!

But Custer had not waited, and Major Marcus Reno and his little command of a hundred and twelve men were fighting for their lives.

Suddenly, and just as the sweating, frightened men thought the red foe was fading back, was giving away, Bloody Knife again pointed dramatically down the val-ley.

"Hunkpapa!" he shouted. "Heap many!"

Out of the tipis at the upper end of the great village now streamed a new horde of painted, half-naked horsemen. Lonesome Charley Reynolds at once drove his pony to the side of Major Reno. He told the white officer that he must instantly begin to fall back toward Custer. But once more his advice was delayed too long. The Hunkpapa horsemen, led by Chief Gall, had al-ready cut around the left flank of Reno's line of troopers. The soldiers on that side were beginning to retreat before the mighty Hunkpapa fighter. In a moment they would be running, not just retreating, and then the Indians would be able to shoot them down like galloping buffalo, helpless, pitiful.

"What can we do, Reynolds?" cried Reno. "I can't hold those men from breaking over there."

Lonesome Charley called to Bloody Knife in the Sioux tongue, and the two scouts spoke swiftly, back and forth.

"Bloody Knife says you must fight your way to those trees in the bend of the river," the white scout told Reno. "If you can get into the trees, the Sioux won't charge you like they will out here in the open grass."

"Someone must go and tell Moylan over there on the left," answered Reno. "We must not start away without telling him."

"I'll go," volunteered Lonesome Charley. "Bloody Knife can stay with you."

The white scout spurred his pony away.

The next moment, the Sioux had renewed their attack upon the middle of Reno's thin line of riflemen, and upon the right flank of the line, where Captain French commanded.

The first of the Seventh Cavalry's soldiers began to fall from their rearing, plunging horses. Against the one hundred and twelve men of the Reno battalion there were now no less than *ten* hundred hostile Indians riding in vengeful fury.

In ten minutes of blasting gunfire, Reno's command suffered eight dead and seven badly wounded.

The troopers were beginning to panic.

Where was Lonesome Charley Reynolds? Why hadn't Captain Moylan come in from the left flank as ordered?

Were they all dead over there?

Major Reno could not answer these terrible questions. He waited as long as any officer would dare to wait for the white scout to return, or for Moylan's troops to appear. Then he turned and told Lieutenant McIntosh that they must go without the others.

"I'm sorry, McIntosh," he said. "But we must leave them."

The young lieutenant answered him with an angry, accusing look. He said nothing, only wheeling and ordering the men to get their horses and be ready to go *fast*.

Reno watched the youthful officer without anger of his own.

He knew McIntosh believed him to be a coward.

To Bloody Knife who stood beside him, he said quietly, "Do you agree with the young man, my friend?"

The faithful Ree scout shook his head, dark eyes flashing.

"Him easy be brave," he said. "Much hard lead retreat."

29. MAJOR RENO'S RACE FOR THE RIVER

Major Reno started his troopers toward the trees in the river's bend. When the soldiers were moving, he left the lead and went back to encourage the stragglers in the rear.

The men were dismounted now, leading their horses. In this way they would not offer such inviting targets for the howling red marksmen. The Indians were riding in so close by this time that the white soldiers could see the sunlight strike the gleaming teeth in their dark faces, as they cursed the white man, firing again and again into the ranks of his desperate retreat. It was a moment to break nerves apart.

But Bloody Knife's great calmness and remarkable bravery helped the terrified troopers to steady down and stay together.

The Ree scout would not get off his pony. He kept the little animal between Major Reno and the war-hooping enemy, thus sheltering the white commander with his body and that of his horse. He had been told by Yellow Hair Custer to go with the Oak Leaf Chief, Reno. This was his duty. He would perform it to the death. And that death now struck him. A Sioux bullet screamed in out of the rolling gunsmoke. It burst against the Ree's head, showering his blood down upon Reno. The startled officer cried out and staggered back as the stricken body of the Indian scout crashed down upon him.

For a moment he did not appear to realize what had happened.

He seemed to be paralyzed by the death of the Ree scout. He could not give commands. Lieutenant McIntosh, little more than a boy in years, rushed up and shouted for the men to remain calm, not to panic and begin running.

"Every fourth man will lead four horses," he ordered. "The other three men, thus freed, will fire their rifles as we retreat toward the river timber. Yonder comes Captain Moylan's troop, men! We are all together now. Let's go, lead out!"

The men ran stumbling and firing back toward the Indians.

The Sioux rushed in behind them, returning the fire. The nearest Indians were less than a stone's toss away. In those last few yards they were not firing, but were trying to get up close enough to the fleeing soldiers to use their war axes and buffalo lances upon them.

Major Reno was among the last three men of his command to reach the trees in the river's bend. Before he could get under cover, White Bull, a great Sioux warrior and nephew of Sitting Bull, ran his pony up behind the white officer and struck him with a war axe. Reno went down, and did not move.

In a display of great bravery, young Lieutenant McIntosh ran out and dragged his commander into the cottonwoods.

The troopers, somewhat protected now, began to get a hard fire into the yelling, wheeling Indians. The red horsemen were packed so closely together that the bullets of the cavalrymen took a heavy toll among them, and very quickly.

First Chief Gall, and then White Bull, called their Hunkpapa away from the cornered Pony Soldiers. The warriors withdrew out of pointblank rifle range. For a precious few minutes Reno's shattered troops could gather their wits and their courage. In the brief lull, during which the Indians continued to fire constantly from long range, the major recovered consciousness.

His first act was to call for Lonesome Charley

Reynolds.

With Bloody Knife gone, the white scout was the only one left to counsel troops in escaping the Sioux trap.

But Dr. De Wolf, one of the regimental surgeons, who was bandaging Reno's scalp-wound, shook his head.

"I'm sorry, Major," he said. "Reynolds is dead. He was killed after he carried your retreat order to Moylan. We also lost six more troopers getting over here into these trees. Hold still, please, sir. You must let me finish."

Reno staggered to his feet, pushing the doctor away.

"Moylan!" he shouted. "Moylan, where are you?"

Captain Myles Moylan, happy-go-lucky Irishman and Reno's second-in-command, came up through the drifting powder-smoke.

"Yes sir," he saluted. Although his face was blackened with grease and powder-grime, and dried blood stained his blue blouse, he was still grinning, still fighting. "What can I do for you, Major? Would you like thirty days leave?"

Reno was a man without much humor. He did not smile now at the Irish captain's small joke.

"Moylan," he said, "tell the other officers we are going to run for the bluffs across the river. Have every man get to his horse and mount-up immediately. We have a moment now while the Indians are readying for their final rush. That's an order, Moylan. Hurry. We have no other chance."

So it came about that Major Reno made the fateful decision to strike across the Little Big Horn and try to reach high ground. His men were remounted and galloping out of the cottonwoods for the crossing of the stream before Gall and White Bull realized their intention. Then the Indians came after them in a great whooping charge of blazing Winchesters and neighing, lunging war ponies.

There were less than one hundred soldiers now.

Many of those remaining were wounded, or without weapons.

Behind them came the hundreds upon hundreds of

the war-bonneted Hunkpapa Sioux, screaming their hoarse-throated war cries. It did not seem to the white-faced, sweaty and blood-stained troopers of Reno's battalion that any of them would ever reach the river alive.

30. "BENTEEN, COME QUICK—
BRING PACKS—!"

General Custer led his troops away through the hills toward the lower end of the great Indian village. His orders were for a fast trot and no bugle calls or other unnecessary noise. When one of his officers rode up beside him to question the matter of leaving Reno without the promised support, the General laughed happily, thin face flushed with excitement.

"What better support can I give him than to strike these rascals on one end, while he smites them on the other?" he cried. "Don't you remember how it worked on the Washita, sir?"

The officer saluted and said nothing.

He remembered all too well how it had worked on the Washita. On the Washita, Custer had abandoned Colonel Elliott much as he had just now left Major Reno —without advising either commander of his change-of-plan.

Returning to his own troop, the officer prayed that *this* time the strategy would work less tragically.

But if some in those five troops of Seventh Cavalry now jingling rapidly through the rough hills beyond the Little Big Horn knew doubt of their leader's wisdom, there were many more who still had complete faith therein.

None of these felt a greater trust in the General than Custer's young favorite, Trumpeter John Martin.

Johnny Martin, the regimental bugler boy, was not yet twenty years old. Born in faraway Italy, young

Martin—his name had been "Martini"—could neither speak nor understand English too well. But he loved his new country and he worshiped General George Armstrong Custer.

Riding now at the General's side, the immigrant boy reflected the prevailing attitude of his fellow-troopers in the Seventh Cavalry. They were tired from the long night march which had brought them to the Indian camp. They wished the General might have waited one more day and permitted them to rest up for the fight. But they had no fear and no doubt of their commanding officer's ability to whip the Sioux.

If the General said that now was the time to hit the red devils, then "forward, ho!" and get the job over with!

Presently the column turned to its left. Custer had seen a high place up on the river's bluffs. The view should be splendid from up there, giving a long sighting of the valley and of the enemy village.

He was right as usual.

When the command halted behind the edge of the high bluff, young Johnny Martin went forward with General Custer and Adjutant Cooke to the very lip of the yellow clay cliff.

Below them the huge hostile encampment spread along the opposite side of the river. To the surprise of the bugler boy the Indians did not seem to be stirring or aroused. He could see the distant tiny brown dots of the figures moving about their camp chores without haste. As if to confirm the boy's thoughts, General Custer, who had been examining the village through his field glasses, put down the glasses and turned to Adjutant Cooke, voice crackling.

"Lieutenant!" he said triumphantly, "we have got them this time——!"

Lieutenant Cooke, the adjutant, seemed to frown slightly. Johnny Martin wondered if he were worried about something.

"Will we wait here for Reno to attack?" Cooke asked. "Or go on?"

Again Custer laughed happily.

"Wait?" he said. "Listen—" He held up a fringed gauntlet, cocking his head up the valley. "Don't you hear that?"

As Cooke strained to hear, so did bugler boy Martin.

Whatever it was that Custer had heard, or that his adjutant, Lieutenant Cooke, now heard, Johnny Martin heard nothing. The wind was moving away from them, and the immigrant boy could not identify the distant "pipping noise" which came to them there on the high bluff. But it was a sound both Custer and Cooke knew all too well.

"There's your answer!" cried the General. "Let's go!"

The command turned back from the bluff. The pace was the gallop now. They had come two miles from leaving Reno to his fate. They sped now a third mile before coming to a long ravine which split the bluffs and led downward steeply to the river. Here Custer once more halted the five troops.

"Trumpeter!" he called to Trooper Martin. "I want you to take a message to Captain Benteen. Ride as fast as you can and tell him to hurry. It's a big village, and I want him to be quick and to bring the ammunition packs."

The boy saluted and turned to depart.

"Wait!" called Adjutant Cooke. The young officer knew that the bugler boy spoke poor English, and might mix up the vital message to Benteen. "I will write that order down for you, Johnny."

He took a note-pad and hurriedly scribbled the message to Captain Benteen which was to become one of the most famed documents in American frontier history. Handing the small piece of paper to Trumpeter Martin, he put his hand on the boy's shoulder, spoke very seriously.

"Now, Johnny," he said, "ride as fast as you can to Captain Benteen. Take the same trail we came down. If you have time, and there is no danger, come back. But otherwise stay with your company."

Johnny Martin saluted again, and turned his horse.

In a few minutes he passed the high bluff where Custer had viewed the camp. And where, perhaps—no man will ever know—he and Lieutenant Cooke had heard the distant sounds of Reno's battalion firing at the overwhelming Sioux.

The boy spoke to his galloping brown horse, encouraging him to more speed. For now, to Trumpeter Martin's *own* ears, the sounds of Major Reno's desperate rifle-fire was coming, and in a continuous, unmistakable crackling volley.

"Run hard, horse!" shouted the immigrant youth in his native tongue. "Something very bad is happening!"

Before long, Johnny Martin came again to the valley of the Little Big Horn. His heart leaped. Out across the meadow, coming from the far side, he saw a column of horsemen riding in troop formation. These must be soldiers! No Indians rode together like that. The bugler boy spurred his mount over the open grasslands, standing in his stirrups and crying out for the soldiers to wait. Hearing him, the officer at the head of the galloping column halted his troops.

Johnny Martin slid his weary mount to a halt, a prayer of thanks on his lips. He had found Captain Benteen!

When Benteen had read the message from Custer, he handed it silently to his fellow officers, who had just galloped up.

The officers read the hastily scrawled note.

Then they, too, fell silent.

Were these the last words of Yellow Hair Custer?

. . . BENTEEN, COME ON—BIG VILLAGE—
BE QUICK—BRING PACKS. P.S. BRING
PACKS . . .

Benteen folded the paper, put it in his breast pocket "If we are lucky," he said to the waiting officers, "we may just be able to reach Major Reno on the bluff above those trees in the river bend ahead. There is no chance whatever of reaching General Custer *four miles farther down this valley.* Back to your commands, gentlemen. We will run for Reno's position."

Trumpeter Johnny Martin, remembering Lieutenant Cooke's orders should danger threaten, stayed with Captain Benteen.

Thus the angels touched an immigrant boy upon the shoulder.

31. IRON CEDAR SEES THE GRAY HORSE TROOP

Iron Cedar could scarcely believe his eyes.

The great warrior Gall had dispatched him to this high point on the bluff where he could serve as a lookout for more Pony Soldiers, while Gall finished off the frightened troops which had fled the river trees and taken refuge on the hill across the Greasy Grass.

Iron Cedar could not know that these were Major Reno's soldiers which Gall had cornered on the hill. Nor would he have cared. His job was to make sure that no other Pony Soldiers approached to bother the Hunkpapa of Gall and White Bull.

That is why his slanted black eyes were now so wide.

Down from the eastern slopes of the river, away down there by the tipis of the Cheyenne, the Sans Arc, the Oglala and the Minniconjou, *more* Pony Soldiers *were* appearing!

In that far view—three or four miles—even the keen eyesight of an Indian was strained. But Iron Cedar saw that one of the troops coming down from those far hills to threaten the other end of the camp was mounted on light-colored horses. Those could be gray horses. And Iron Cedar, and every Sioux warrior of note, knew with which leader rode the Gray Horse Troop of the Seventh Calvary. *That was Yellow Hair Custer coming down from those far hills!*

Now, surely, Iron Cedar must report such an exciting thing to Chief Gall and the Hunkpapa. Even though the other Pony Soldiers were not in a place to interfere with the finishing of the soldiers trapped on the hill, would not Gall want to know where Yellow Hair was? Would he want all the glory of fighting Custer to fall to the Cheyenne? Or even to his own Sioux brothers of the Oglala or Minniconjou bands?

Iho! It was hardly possible.

Away went Iron Cedar, sweeping down into the valley on his fleet pony. Racing up to Gall, he gave him the news. Gall and White Bull had almost gotten the soldiers on the hill down to their last bullets. They could tell this by the reduced rifle-fire of the surrounded troopers. In a few more minutes those trapped Pony Soldiers would all be killed. But also in a few more minutes, the Cheyenne or Oglala or Minniconjou might have met and defeated Yellow Hair! That would never do.

With a wild yell, Gall called his best fighters to him.

Down the grassy valley the Hunkpapa drove their ponies, war cries echoing. Many others of White Bull's warriors also went with the Hunkpapa chief to be in on the killing of Yellow Hair.

On the hill above, Reno's soldiers, doomed but the moment before, saw the Indians leaving them to race off upvalley. The weary, sweat-stained troopers rose from their shallow-dug rifle-pits and hiding-holes, giving thanks to God. In the same moment of divine help, they saw Captain Benteen's column leave the far side of the valley and gallop toward their side.

The troopers could not know that Trumpeter Martin had just found Benteen with Custer's last message. Neither could they know that Benteen had decided to stay with Reno on the hill, and was even then rushing over the meadow to join them. The troopers with Reno would never know, either, that it was Iron Cedar's message to Chief Gall which was just as fateful as Johnny Martin's ride from Custer. And perhaps even more so.

For if the Hunkpapa had not been called away by Gall's jealous pride to make certain that Crazy Horse, Crow King, Bob-Tail-Horse, Roan Bear and the other famed war chiefs did not grasp all the credit for destroying Yellow Hair, Benteen could never have crossed the valley and lived. Or, had he done so by bloody sacrifice, he would have found no single trooper of Major Reno's command still alive to greet him.

But the heart-felt cheers of the Reno survivors which met Benteen's exhausted but uninjured command were stilled almost as they rose from the parched throats of the rescued.

Even as Benteen's troopers, with the pack train of mules bearing the desperately needed ammunition, fought their ways up the hill through the remaining Sioux, a great quiet fell upon the valley. The Indians, themselves, stopped firing.

Far down along the river, borne upward faintly upon a rising current of the afternoon air, came the sound of thin and ragged rifle-fire. And it was not Winchester fire. Those were Springfield carbines firing. Seventh Cavalry guns.

"God help us," said a white-faced trooper softly. "That's the General down there. They have got him . . ."

32. "THERE WAS NOT TIME TO LIGHT A PIPE . . ."

Custer began the descent to the river. Adjutant Cooke, looking at his pocket watch, noted the hour: 3:30 P.M. An air of tense confidence was shared now by officer and man.

The General had caught the lower camp napping.

With his swift wide circle out away from the stream, he had completed the same fatal surprise tactic with which he had destroyed the camp of Black Kettle on the Washita.

All that remained was for his troops to press down the wide gully ahead, charge over the river, unite with the troops of Benteen which must soon appear on the other side. Then the combined commands would turn and drive through the helpless Indians to meet the troops of Reno. The camp would be split in two parts, the people put into panicky flight, the warriors forced to surrender. The victory would be Custer's. And, with the victory, who knew what other prizes?

What actually followed is known only to Indian eyes. Red tongues, alone, can tell the tale.

Custer, the Indians say, came down the slope nearly to the Little Big Horn. The place was at the fording of the river where Medicine Trail Creek enters the mother stream.

It was a true thing, also, that the camp at the lower end was helpless. Most of the warriors had rushed off up the river to help the Hunkpapa kill the Pony Soldiers of Reno. If Yellow Hair had come on down that slope and charged the camp, the Indians would have fled in wild fright, ending the battle. But then a strange thing happened.

Four Cheyenne warriors appeared in full fighting dress.

They were Bob-Tail-Horse, Roan Bean, Calf and another whose name was never remembered. In all of the confusion of running squaws, crying children and frightened old people caused by the sudden appearance of the dreaded Yellow Hair, these four Cheyenne rode straight out toward the ford, and toward the five troops of Custer's Seventh Cavalry.

For a reason no man was ever to know, the supreme courage of the four warriors riding directly into his troops brought Custer to a halt. He ordered the cavalry to stop on the lower slope of the hill, before ever they reached the river.

It was probable that Yellow Hair believed the four Cheyenne were only the tempting bait in an ambush of a hundred times their number of warriors waiting hidden behind the lodges. In any event, his halt upon the hill was a terrible mistake. It permitted Iron Cedar the time to see the Gray Horse Troop from afar. And it gave Gall and White Bull time to bring their Hunkpapa down from the Reno fight. Thus, when the General did order the advance resumed, there were hundreds of warriors in front of him, and he could not get across the ford.

Indeed, he never reached it. The hills all about were suddenly black and swarming with Sioux and, before the Seventh could retreat, half of Custer's command lay dead or wounded on the lower slope. The surviving troops were huddled about their commander midway of the hillside. They cursed their Springfield carbines, and threw them away, and fought on foot with the big Colt revolvers. Ammunition was nearly gone. With every burst of Indian fire, white men fell.

Custer stood hatless in the June sunlight.

His golden curls glinted.

In his hands was his beautifully engraved rifle. Again

and again he fired with it. Each time an Indian screamed, whirled around, pitched from his rearing pony and lay still.

Others of the officers and men of the Seventh Cavalry did what they might. Only heroes were left now upon that bloody hill. The unsure, the weak, the faint, had died in the first wild assault of the Sioux.

Now only Yellow Hair and 115 of his 231 troops, scouts and civilian followers remained.

Upon the north hill a lean warrior wearing a single eagle feather and a black wolfskin cape directed the fighting. Who could miss that handsome face? The panther's grace and fearlessness? It was Tashunka Witko, Crazy Horse, who was tearing at Yellow Hair's left flank. He, and his Oglala.

To the south, the gully was not so much one channel but a series of rough breaks and shallow dips in the hillside. Here were the Hunkpapa, led now by Gall and White Bull, and the Cheyenne with Bob-Tail-Horse, Two Moons and the rest.

In front of Custer the lower slope crawled with Minniconjou and Sans Arc Sioux and with a mixture of all-comers and all bands—in total, some two thousand warriors at this late stage in the fight.

Strangely, now, perhaps in wonderment at the courage of the Pony Soldiers, the host of Indian braves rested their fire, watching Yellow Hair and all that was left of the Gray Horse Troop—the last of the gallant Seventh Cavalry alive upon the upper slope.

In the lull, Custer called his officers and his men to him. He was not yet wounded, although caked with filth and powder grime, as were all the troopers who came now to his call. Those who were not dripping and dark-stained with their own life blood, were covered with the blood of comrades no longer there. As those in the inner ring, near the General, listened to his words, those upon the outside of the circle kept firing to hold the Indians back.

Custer's head was high.

His voice was firm. He raised it scarcely a tone. He spoke to the men as comrades, as brothers-in-arms, and not as a commanding officer to troops about to die.

"Boys," he said, standing straight as the shaft of a buffalo lance, "we are going to reach the top of this hill. We are going up there, and you know why. Let us go like men—like Seventh Cavalrymen—and we shall all meet again upon the other side. God bless you. God keep you all . . ."

Some of the men were weeping.

Others stood for that small instant of eternity there in the sunlit stillness above the Greasy Grass, dry-eyed, but filled with the fierce sharp pain of pride.

They could not speak, could not reply to Custer. Nor were they given time to do so by the Sioux.

A tremendous burst of renewed Indian rifle-fire came from the command of Crazy Horse upon the north hill. With the furious rifle-fire came a thousand-throated scream, and the great mass of Oglala horsemen swept in toward Yellow Hair and his remaining men. Upward the valiant survivors fought their way on foot. But with every step of the way, soldiers fell and did not rise again. When Custer began that last retreat up the slope, he had one hundred and twelve troopers with him. When he came to bay just below the hilltop he had struggled to reach, less than sixty men still stood in a desperate ring about their gallant leader.

Half a hundred lives had been lost within ten minutes.

All there with Custer in that panting, smoke-grimed circle knew that Yellow Hair and the Seventh Cavalry had come to the last stand. But the General's fiery heart would not falter.

His unforgettable voice rose above the battle one more time.

"Stay together, men!" he called. "We are almost to the top. See there where the sun strikes the grass of the crest!"

But the sun was setting for the Seventh Cavalry.

With a final wolf-pack howling of war cries, Crazy Horse and four hundred Oglala warriors drove their painted ponies in upon the huddled knot of white troopers. From the opposite side, Gall swept in with the Cheyenne and the Hunkpapa. The last of the Seventh disappeared beneath the shrieking red wave. In the very center of the Indian tide, Yellow Hair Custer, shot through the breast and bleeding from the mouth, struggled once more to his feet. His big Colt revolver was in his right hand. He fired one, twice, three times. A swinging Oglala war club struck his shoulder, knocking him backward over a dead mount of the Gray Horse Troop. He again reeled upright, then fell to his knees, the big Colt leveled across the body of the gray horse. Suddenly he saw the Indian ponies blot out the sky above him, and then the dark red faces snarling down. He fired upward into the dark faces and into the bodies of the leaping ponies, and that is all that he was aware of —and that is the way that he was found—with his revolver empty and still aimed at the enemy—a Sioux bullethole through his left temple and into his brain.

It was just a little after four o'clock in the afternoon.

Custer's great fight upon the eastern slopes of that far river called the Greasy Grass was over in less than an hour.

As for the final end, that dark moment of the charge of Crazy Horse and his Four Hundred, only an Indian could know how swift was Yellow Hair's last thought.

"After that," the old warriors say, "the fight did not last long enough to light a pipe . . ."

33. SILENT LIES THE SEVENTH

"Sir," said Captain Weir to the wounded Major Reno, "for the final time I beg of you to permit me to take D Troop and go down toward that firing."

The captain was speaking of the distant rifle-fire which many of the Seventh Cavalrymen on Reno's hill believed to be from General Custer. The time was then nearing four o'clock. Most of the attacking Indians were still away down the river with Gall and White Bull. There might yet be a chance that a single troop could slip from the hill and make a scout for Custer and his five troops before the hostiles returned.

But the wound in Major Reno's head made him dizzy and faint. He could not command his senses clearly. For the past hour Captain Benteen had been in actual charge of the defenses. It was the latter who now urged the suffering Reno to grant Weir's request, "before the cursed Sioux come back at us in force."

Reno refused. He insisted that no man leave the hill. If they could defend their position only until nightfall, they might survive. Tomorrow was the twenty-sixth, the date when Gibbon and Terry were due to arrive. Surely, with first sunlight, they would hear the buglers' calls, see the pennants flying.

Weir and Benteen exchanged hopeless glances.

"Major Reno, sir!" repeated brave young Captain Weir, "did you hear me, sir? For the last time, please! Give me your permission to take D Troop and make a scout for the General."

But Reno only pressed the bloody bandage on his

head and groaned. Benteen, standing nearby, looked at Weir and shook his head. It was no use. The major was not listening.

Captain Weir leaned down to face Reno, who was sitting on the ground propped up against a stack of pack-saddles.

"Major, I am going now. You cannot stop me. If you will not authorize me to take D Troop, I will go alone. I, and any man brave enough to come with me."

Reno finally looked up at him.

"I forbid you, or any man, to leave this hill," he said.

But Captain Weir only turned his back and went to where his horse was standing. His lieutenant, a youth named Edgerly, ran up to him and begged to go with him. But Weir told him he was now in command of D Troop, in Weir's place, and must remain with the men. Before the young officer could reply, the captain put spurs to his mount and dashed off the hill and down the spine of the long ridge which led toward the lower Indian camp, and toward the sound of the distant rifle-fire.

Yet when Captain Weir could defy Reno out of loyalty to General Custer, then why could not Lieutenant Edgerly disobey Captain Weir for the same reason?

Two tough sergeants came up to the youthful officer, seeing him start for his horse.

"What do you think you're going to do, Lieutenant?" they asked. "Follow the Captain?"

"You two men stay here and hold the troop together," answered Edgerly. "There will be no officers when I am gone."

"Yes, sir," saluted the two hard-faced sergeants. "You can surely trust us, sir. Can't he, boys?"

The question went to the weary, powder-burned troopers of D Troop who were now coming up to see what was going on.

"Oh, yes sir!" chorused the soldiers. "We wouldn't think of following the Lieutenant when he follows the Captain!"

Edgerly turned and rode off after Captain Weir.

Immediately the two sergeants swung to their saddles.

"D Troop, mount up!" bawled one of them, and the valiant men ran for their tethered horses and got to saddle.

"Forward, ho, D Troop!" shouted the other sergeant, and away down the ridge went every able-bodied trooper in the company of Captain Weir and Lieutenant Edgerly. The two officers, hearing hoofbeats, turned in their saddles. But what could they say? What could any officers say to men like that? What could be said, was said by Captain Weir in a voice that was choked with feeling.

"All right . . . God bless you, boys," he said. "Let's go and find the General——!"

But they were not to find Custer that day.

They advanced down the ridge as far as they could, being shot at by Indians every step of the way. And being in danger of being cut off and killed to the man at any moment.

Finally they could ride no farther.

A mile or more away they saw a sunlit, silent slope of the river where many Indians were riding around and around on their ponies shooting arrows and rifles into some motionless objects on the ground. They could hear no other fire now than that coming from the sharp bark of the red men's Winchesters.

But there was no fight going on upon that distant field.

If the firing they had heard before had been that of Custer, then Custer was no longer on that field.

Had he been there?

If so, where was he now?

Weir and Edgerly discussed the matter with their sergeants.

None of them mentioned the possibility of a defeat for the General. It was agreed that Custer had found the Sioux too strong for his small force, and turned back. Most probably he was making another circle to find

General Gibbon or General Terry and rush with them back to help Reno and Benteen.

They even took cheer in the notion that the General would soon come charging back up the valley with reinforcements.

But the Indians were now leaving the sunlit slope in the distance and returning toward Reno's hill. Weir and Edgerly started back, but were frightened to learn that the Sioux had gotten behind them. Were they cut off?

Only the fact that cool Captain Benteen now appeared leading a column of troopers along the ridge toward them saved their lives. Joining up with Benteen, the combined troops fought their way back to the hill, and the fortifications they had dug there. There the fight raged anew, its red fires raised up again by the return of Gall and the Hunkpapa, and of Crazy Horse and the Oglala, and of Two Moons and the Cheyenne. Suddenly it seemed to the troopers on the hill that all of the Indians in Montana were charging at them up every side and slope of their high bluff. They were saved only by the fact that darkness fell, and the Indians went back to their camps to light the victory fires and start the scalp-dances. The men on the blackened hill tried not to think about where those scalps might have been taken that day.

All night long the wild fires leaped and the war drums boomed in the great hostile encampment.

But there was no rest for the soldiers on the hill.

Hour after hour Benteen and Weir and Moylan and the other officers drove them to the task of scraping more rifle-pits in the flinty earth of the bluff-top. They used spoons, tin cups, spurs, knives, their fingernails —anything with which they could dig a shallow depression which might hide their bodies from the Indian bullets which sunrise would surely bring in blazing showers. The only real tools on the hill were three spades and two axes brought in by the pack train. All of the horses and mules were put in the center of the circle of shallow rifle-pits and tied there so that they could not

be stampeded by the Indian fire. When the first streaks
of the summer dawn of June 26th lighted the east
Captain Benteen went to Major Reno, and crouched
beside him.

"Marc," he said, "we've done all we can. Before they
beat us, they will know they've tangled with the Seventh
Cavalry." He paused, looking off through the gloom.
"What do you suppose has become of Custer?" he asked.

Reno shook his head, but then spoke hopefully.

"I think he is all right. He will be coming into our line
as soon as the daylight lets him see where we are."

"No," said Benteen, "you're wrong, Marc. The talk
among the men is that he's gone on and deserted us.
They are cursing him plenty, believe me. As for myself,
well, you know what I think of the General."

"Yes, I know," answered Reno softly. "But it is you
who are wrong. Custer would never leave us."

"Oh? What was it he did to Major Elliott on the
Washita?"

"Elliott was dead. Custer knew that."

"We all knew it—later on."

"Please go and have one more look to the lines,"
ordered Reno, straightening. "They will be back at us
any moment."

Even as he spoke, the day broke over the eastern hills
and the Sioux were screaming their war cries and once
more forcing their ponies up the slopes of the bluff.

Soon they stopped charging and took sheltered places
from which they fired into the soldier positions on top of
the hill. Hour after hour the fire continued. And every
hour more soldiers died, more were torn by wounds,
more began to lose all hope and to pray for a merciful,
quick death.

Then a strange and uneasy thing commenced to occur
among the Indians. The soldiers began to hear the
blowing of cavalry bugles down in the war camp.
Straining to see, they made out some of the half-naked
warriors riding about tooting the trumpets. Others of
the red warriors were wearing uniforms and parts of

uniforms of U.S. Cavalry troopers. Here and there an officer's hat was seen, or a blue coat with gold epaulets on the shoulders. Where had the Sioux gotten these things?

It was a dark question, and the men upon the hill would not try to answer it.

The fight continued all that day, the Indians charging the hill, the soldiers pushing them back, but always the action ending with the red men dug in a little nearer to the hill's top than they had been before.

With the second darkness the soldiers buried their dead and moved their rifle-pit positions into a smaller circle. This was very easy, now, for there were so few to dig for, and so few to hide. Volunteer patrols stole down to the river to bear up water that the dying might drink, and the living might drink also, and so live a little longer.

They knew now that Custer was not coming.

Or that when he came he would be too late.

One more hard charge by the hostiles in the morning and the Seventh Cavalry would be no more.

But that charge never came. Unknown to the men upon the hill, the column of Terry and Gibbon had been sighted by the Indian scouts late that second afternoon. Even as the warriors were making their last wild rides to overrun the hilltop, the squaws were taking down the lodges and the young boys were running in the vast pony herds. When daylight of June 27th dawned pale and clear, it revealed to the wounded heroes on the hill two sights of equal joy and wonder.

Far to the southeast, fingering off through the hills of the Rosebud and of the Greasy Grass, the black lines of the retreating Indian camp crawled like distant, fleeing ants.

Nearer at hand—much nearer—marching up the river from the north, came the long blue lines of the United States Infantry. Their bright pennants fluttered in the morning sun. The brass notes of their bugles blended with the hoarse braying of the pack mules and the rumble of artillery wheels.

The sleepless Seventh Cavalrymen watching from th
weathered bluffs above the deserted hostile camp stoc
and cheered to the man, tears streaming down the
gaunt faces.

These were the troops of Red Nose Gibbon an
General Terry, come at last!

Reno and Benteen were saved.

The Sioux were scattered to a thousand prairie wind
But wait.

Where was Custer? What had happened to Yello
Hair?

The question was answered an hour later when a
advance scout from Gibbon rode up to the rifle barr
cades on Reno Hill.

General Custer and all of his five troops of th
Seventh U.S. Cavalry had been found upon a gras
slope four miles below—every officer and man strippe
naked, lying still-eyed and silent in the summer su
light, at peace forever along the banks of the Little B
Horn.

34. CRAZY HORSE COMES IN

For nine months following the destruction of the Seventh Cavalry, the Sioux of Sitting Bull and of Crazy Horse wandered the outer plains like lonesome wolves.

The Cheyenne had left them. Two Moons, Dull Knife and the other principal chiefs were talking peace. They said that the white man would surely come with more new Pony Soldiers than a cloud of locusts to avenge the death of Yellow Hair. And there were many rumors and stories flying about the prairie to support such fears.

American Horse, the great Oglala, had been killed . . . His forty-eight lodges had been burned . . . Three Stars Crook was back up from Wyoming . . . General Nelson A. Miles, "Bear Coat" Miles, was marching up the Yellowstone with a huge force . . . Red Cloud had been removed from power by the white man . . . Spotted Tail was now the head chief of the agency Indians.

Then, late in the autumn, came news of a terrible blow to the wild Sioux. The Cheyenne had been broken in battle.

General Mackenzie had captured and burned to the snows the main village of Dull Knife, head chief of all the Cheyenne. In the fight, the war chief, Last Bull, leader of the fierce Cheyenne Dog Soldiers—the tribe's best fighters—had been killed. Dull Knife had surrendered to the whites. Little Wolf, that unforgiving warrior, had fled with the few Cheyenne survivors who would not surrender to live on an agency.

But when Little Wolf sought to join his people with

the Oglala of Crazy Horse, Crazy Horse turned him
away.

Yes! it was true.

Tashunka Witko, fighter of fighters against the white
man, had said that he would now go in. The defeat of his
old friend Dull Knife had decided him. Crazy Horse was
taking final counsel with his fellow Sioux, even then,
before sending word to the agency and to Spotted Tail
that the Oglala were ready to surrender "when the new
grass comes again."

Angered, Little Wolf returned to the agency and
offered his services, and those of his free Cheyenne, as
scouts to help the soldiers hunt down Crazy Horse and
Sitting Bull!

It was the beginning of the end, when Indian thus
turned upon Indian. The melting of the snows would
finish the red man.

Many of the Sioux could not believe these tales.
When spring did come at last, they traveled to the
village of Tashunka Witko to hear the words from the
war chief's own lips. When they arrived, they heard
even more than they had been told of bad news.

Not only was Crazy Horse going to surrender, but
Sitting Bull had fled the country!

Iho! it was a true thing.

With two hundred lodges of his Hunkpapa people,
and some of the Oglala people who would not go in with
Crazy Horse, the vision-dreamer of the Little Big Horn
had escaped northward into Canada, "the Land of the
Grandmother."

There the hated Pony Soldiers could not follow them.

There they would try to make a life like the old free
life in the United States. It was better than slavery. It
was better than starving on a reservation. *Woyuonihan!*

Unable to believe their ears, the visiting Sioux gathered at the great red and black lodge of Crazy Horse to
hear his final speech.

They knew, as they came there, that Spotted Tail had
been there before them. The old man had come from the

agency to plead with his hostile brothers to give up the hopeless fight. He was gone back, now, afraid to linger too long among the wild and fierce Oglala. This speech of Tashunka Witko's which they now would hear was the war chief's answer to the old man's plea for peace.

What would he say? What would his Oglala people do?

"My brothers," began the dark-skinned warrior-hero, "our Uncle Spotted Tail has told me there is no use to fight any more. We have no remaining chance to beat the Pony Soldiers. But what I say here is for myself. All of you must do what your own hearts say to do."

He paused, the firelight marking his sorrowful face.

"I have fought long," he resumed, "and I love this Land of the Spotted Eagle. But I am tired, and the soldiers are too many now. I am all done. I am going in. I have asked our Uncle Sitting Bull if he would surrender with me. He said that he would not. That he did not wish to die just yet. He has gone to the Land of the Grandmother. His trail is broad and easy to see. Those of you who wish to may follow it. But my home is here on this Montana soil, and to the east, in the *Pa Sapa* sacred to our fathers. I will not run away. I am going in to the agency. I gave my promise to follow Spotted Tail along the road to peace."

The Sioux went away and smoked their pipes and thought of the decision to be made.

Next morning all of the lodges came down. Half of them traveled to the east, toward the agency, with Crazy Horse. The other half went to the north, toward Canada and the people of Sitting Bull.

For four moons, May to September, Crazy Horse lived without trouble at Red Cloud agency. Then his beloved wife, Black Blanket, sickened. The warchief was arrested while trying to take her to the doctor at nearby Spotted Tail agency. He was escorted under guard back to Red Cloud by Major Jesse M. Lee, agent at Spotted Tail and a true friend of the red man.

As twilight drew down, they approached the agency

with its soldier barracks and bayonet-armed sentries. Major Lee for the final time warned the great warrior to be careful, that there could be grave danger for him here.

Crazy Horse only nodded and continued riding straight toward the agency. It was dark when he got down from his horse and shook hands with the soldier chief who met him outside the office of General Bradley, who commanded the troops at the agency.

The soldier chief seemed very nervous.

The Indians sensed the officer's uncertainty. The best friends of Crazy Horse among them came to stand by the proud Oglala war chief. They were Swift Bear, Touch-the-Clouds, High Bear, Black Crow and Good Voice. They looked hard at the officer.

"Excuse me," said the latter hurriedly to Crazy Horse. "I will tell General Bradley that you are here."

When he came back out of the general's office, his face was drawn tight. His eyes would not look at the Indians.

"The General says that if you will come with me," he instructed Crazy Horse, "not a hair of your head will be harmed."

The war chief hesitated. He looked at his friends. They shook their heads quickly, for they were suspicious now.

But Tashunka Witko was not afraid.

He shook hands with the soldiers who had marched up suddenly to escort him. But he had no idea that the little building toward which the soldiers then took him was the guardhouse of the agency troops—the jail.

When he saw the iron-bound door swing open, revealing the bars of the prison rooms within, he gave a great cry like some wild animal at the closing of the steel trap upon its tortured legs.

Crazy Horse became then like an animal.

He wheeled about and broke free of the soldiers. He had seen the white man's "iron house." No power on earth could put his free wild spirit in such a foul and filthy cage. He ran toward the outer darkness, but only a stride or two.

The bayonet of one of the soldier-guards struck him through the back. He stopped and straightened slowly. Some of his Indian friends took hold of him to help him stand. But he shook his head, deep voice moaning like a hurt beast.

"Let me go, my friends," he said. "Can't you see that I have my last wound . . ."

The Indians took their hands away. They shrank back from him, as coyotes from the growling of the king wolf.

The war chief turned slowly and began to walk toward the soldiers who had bayoneted him. He took three proud steps. Then, without another sound, he slid forward down into the dirt of the prison-yard, shirt and leggins already black with life-blood.

Touch-the-Clouds ran up to his leader's fallen body.

"Let me take him to the lodges of my people," he pleaded with the soldier chief. "You have killed him here. Let him die with his own kind."

"Carry him into the guardhouse!" shouted the soldier chief to the troopers. "And clear this yard at once!"

But Touch-the-Clouds would not move.

He reached down and gently lifted the body of Crazy Horse.

"Where my chief goes, there I go," he told the officer. And, turning, he bore the stricken Oglala toward the iron-bound doorway. The soldiers parted to let him pass. The officer, touched by that Indian dignity which the treachery of the white man had never weakened, bowed his head. Two other figures followed behind Touch-the-Clouds and Crazy Horse. And these, too, the soldiers permitted to pass; they were the aged parents of the dying war chief.

The guards cleared the yard of all other Indians. The post surgeon hurried up through the lamplight. After a while he came out of the guardhouse, and spoke to the waiting officer.

"The bayonet entered both kidneys," he said in a low voice. "There is nothing to do for him."

In a small bare room inside the jail building of the Pony Soldiers at Red Cloud Agency, Crazy Horse lay dying.

There was no bed, only a pile of army blankets upon the cold stone floor.

With their faces to the wall, his parents were crouched praying to the Great Spirit, crying the words of the chant for the Fallen Ones, the Katela Song of the Sioux People.

By the blankets crouched Touch-the-Clouds, his hand holding the hand of his dear friend. He could feel the coldness coming into the dark fingers of the war chief.

"My chief," he said, "is there something you would have me tell the people? Anything at all, Tashunka?"

He saw the slender face move, the lean head nod slightly.

"My brother," whispered Crazy Horse, *"I am bad hurt; tell the people it is no use to depend upon me any more. . . ."*

With those words, he was gone, and the story finished.

Crazy Horse, last war chief of all the Sioux, was in the arms of Wakan Tanka. Sitting Bull, the vision-dreamer, had vanished into Canada. Yellow Hair slept along the Greasy Grass. The war drums thumped no more upon the Powder or the Rosebud. Then, truly, could it be said, and softly:

The Battle of the Little Big Horn was ended.

ABOUT THE AUTHOR

WILL HENRY was born and grew up in Missouri, where he attended Kansas City Junior College. Upon leaving school, he lived and worked throughout the western states, acquiring the background of personal experience reflected later in the realism of his books. Presently residing in California, he writes for motion pictures and television, as well as continuing his research into frontier lore and legend, which are the basis for his unique blend of history and fiction. Four of his novels have been purchased for motion picture production, and several have won top literary awards, including four of the coveted Spur Awards of the Western Writers of America. Mr. Henry's most recent books include: *From Where the Sun Now Stands, The Last Warpath, Reckoning at Yankee Flat,* and *Chiricahua.*